Why Love is not Enough

Sol Gordon, Ph.D.

7-7-00

To Dearest Xiao-Wei,

May the love partner you select reflect your character of caring, thoughtfulness, courage and love.

My love always,
Kuo Hu

COMPLETELY REVISED

Why Love is not Enough

NEW! Intimacy: The new sexuality of the 90s

NEW! Is your relationship ready for marriage?

How to identify the right person for you

The essential factors for a successful relationship

People and relationships you must walk away from
(especially when considering a second marriage)

Sol Gordon, Ph.D.

ADAMS MEDIA CORPORATION
Holbrook, Massachusetts

Published by Adams Media Corporation
260 Center Street, Holbrook, MA 02343

ISBN: 1-55850-850-3

Printed in Canada.

G   H   I   J

This publication is designed to provide accurate and authoritative information
with regard to the subject matter covered. It is sold with the understanding that
the publisher is not engaged in rendering legal, accounting, or other professional advice. If legal advice or other expert assistance is required, the services of a
competent professional person should be sought.
— From a *Declaration of Principles* jointly adopted by a Committee of the
American Bar Association and a Committee of Publishers and Associations

This book is available at quantity discounts for bulk purchases.
For information, call 1-800-872-5627.

Visit our home page at http://www.adamsmedia.com

Dedication

My wife Judith and I recently celebrated our 35th wedding anniversary. Along with our misfortunes, we experienced many joys and great times. My marriage to Judith was the best thing that ever happened to me—and it's still happening!

Judith, thanks for your patience with me; thanks for being yourself. I hope that when we celebrate our 50th anniversary together, we'll look up and say to each other, "I still like you."

Acknowledgments

Many thanks are due to Joey Tranchina and Brandon Toropov for their work on the second edition of this book.

Contents

Introduction

THIS BOOK IS for people who want a lasting, mature relationship. It is also for people whose current relationship or marriage is unsatisfactory.

Perhaps, if you are a woman, you are beginning to believe that all the nice men are either married or gay. The rest (or so the conventional wisdom goes) are all too ugly, too short, too old, too young, too "wimpy," or flat-out insensitive and sex obsessed.

Or, if you are a man, you may be thinking that all the available women are too unattractive, too attractive, too smart, too dumb, too materialistic, or, to quote the ancient (and crude) complaint, "unwilling to put out."

Yet there is someone for just about everyone, and close to 90% of us, it is estimated, marry—eventually. That is certainly an encouraging sign for those eager to enter into a long-term relationship.

In this book, I will encourage you to develop a new attitude. Many of us begin our relationships with others from positions of self-doubt, desperation, and low self-esteem (which, when you think about it, are not the most attractive traits to put forward to a potential partner).

What must you do? First, you must decide that you do want to enter a healthy, enriching relationship, or improve the one you have now. Only then will this book be helpful to you in attaining your goal of a successful match.

By successful I do not mean anything fancy. My definition of a successful relationship is one in which, after the passage of a considerable period of time, the partners can still say to each other, "I like you."

The guidelines in this book are simple; the follow-through, however, will be difficult and will require time and patience. You should also learn to cultivate an outlook that allows you to give new approaches an honest try. You may not agree with some of my suggestions, but you should keep an open mind.

Following are some basic principles that underlie the ideas in this book. They apply whether or not you have been married previously and whether you are a man or a woman.

If you are desperate, you broadcast a negative message. That message makes you unattractive no matter how good you look.

Your feelings of self-worth should not depend on finding someone. If you feel that you will not amount to anything until you "catch" someone for your very own partner, you probably won't amount to much after you do.

Life has not passed you by. No matter what the barriers are (including physical handicap and current or previous troubled relationships), you can find someone who will help you grow into a happier, more complete person.

Sex is not the most important element in a mature relationship. Intimacy is more of an authentic turn-on; of the ten most important aspects of a mature relationship, sex, in my view, ranks ninth.

Some love relationships are mature; others are immature. And it is easier than you might think to tell the difference.

Successful relationships involve compromises and are almost never ideal. They are often enjoyable, but expecting them to be enjoyable all of the time is unrealistic and self-defeating.

Commitment to growth is an essential component of a happy relationship. This means mutual commitment to grow as a couple, as well as to each partner's individual growth.

Marriage must be a rational and intellectually sound decision. If you think that you have found the right person, the best advice is always to think it through once again. There are some people you definitely should not marry. Although powerful feelings of love and sexual attraction often play major roles, a marriage stands little or no chance of succeeding if the essential issues are not thoroughly thought out.

This book offers no guarantee or panacea. Nothing works for everyone, but the approach I offer can help you learn a new, more realistic way of looking at yourself and at your relationships with others.

I wrote this book for intelligent people who are eager to make up their own minds about how to live and what risks are worth taking in relationships. If this describes you, it is worth your while to continue reading.

Together, you and I might make a shiddoch (Yiddish for "marital match or agreement). I am asking you to approach this book with the realization that work is required on your part. My part of this bargain is to provide you with good ideas based upon sound information; yours begins by seeing yourself as a person who is worth spending time with, and then by being ready and willing to try the new approaches that can change your life.

S.G.

Chapter One:
Intimacy and Marriage
in the '90s

SO YOU'RE IN LOVE. That's wonderful—but, for heaven's sake, do not marry for love. The decision to marry should be rationally motivated—and love, even if you're "madly" in love, is not reason enough.

So you're not in love. Don't worry; your turn will come. But, whatever you do, don't marry for status—whether that's the car he drives; the college she attended; the position he holds; the business she owns; his wealth; or the social prestige of her parents.

Whatever you do, don't make sexual electricity your prime criterion. And don't base your decision on any visionary experience you feel must accompany real love. You'd be surprised at the number of excellent relationships (and potentially good marriages) that break up because one of the partners was not sure if it was *love*, where *love* was defined as a kind of craziness, an excitation (like heart palpitations), with side effects ranging from eating disorders to insomnia.

The head-over-heels experience is not uncommon, but it's probably not as meaningful as you think. No couple that has undergone the experience of being "madly in love," Hollywood-style, with swooning, dizzying, passionate sex at sunset, candlelight dinners, and nights filled with sweet dreams of the beloved, can minimize the impact of such infatuation. However, it's important to keep in mind that ecstasy (and social ambition, for that matter) has its time and place—and that many bad marriage decisions have been based on such considerations.

Helena Amram, the famous *shadchen*, or matchmaker, once suggested that "most people are not marriage material." She described many women as married to their careers, and considered some so dominating that they risk overpowering the ordinary man. Many of the men Amram encountered were late bloomers, mama's boys, too selfish to marry, or married to *their* jobs.

In light of a recent headline that appeared in the San Francisco Chronicle ("Most First Marriages Doomed, New Study Says," March 13, 1989), Amram just may be right. My job in this book is to help put the odds in your favor. I don't make blanket promises or blind guarantees; but then again, there are a few things I do know for sure.

For example, I know that if you are desperate, you will invariably attract someone who will hurt or exploit you. And I know that if you feel threatened and suspicious of just about everyone who is caring or expresses tenderness toward you, then you have some problems—problems that may require professional counseling. I also know that if you are true to yourself, and if you respect yourself, someone who is right for you will be attracted to you and will respect you.

This self-knowledge and self-respect is the basis of the authentic turn-on of a genuine relationship.

* * *

Tens of thousands of relationships break up each year because one of the partners remains troubled by the initial "lack of sexual desire" or no longer feels sexually excited. All too often, to paraphrase the Righteous Brothers, once partners lose that loving feeling, the relationship is gone, gone, gone.

Does it have to be that way?

Emily says, "John is wonderful; I love the way we laugh and have lots of fun together. We have similar interests, and he is good looking—at least, that's what my friends say. John is my best friend . . . but he doesn't turn me on. Then there's Jim. I think he drinks too much; he's not as bright as I'd like; he's always late. He can't keep a job, either. But he's gorgeous! He's crazy about me—and wow, does he turn me on!"

Emily is going to marry Jim. What do you think of that? How do you think that decision makes Emily feel about herself?

Sex is greatly exaggerated as a critical factor in a successful marriage. As I often point out, sex ranks only number nine on my list of the ten most important factors in a good long-term relationship.

My message is simple. Don't be a fool; don't marry mainly because of sexual attraction or sex chemistry. This attraction doesn't last very long.

Is there sex after marriage? Of course. Is there romance after marriage? Definitely. But mutual understanding, commitment, trust, and a sense of humor are more significant factors in the survival and success of a marriage. This is the essence of the new intimacy, an intimacy based on reality, not fantasy.

Do not marry for money, beauty, job security, social connections, or because you hear the tick-tock of your biological clock. These factors may be excellent reasons to do many other things besides get married. But if you expect any of these interests to form a foundation for the central relationship of your adult life, you will be disappointed.

Sure: Some people fall madly in love and manage to hold on. Sometimes love at first sight does last. And some dark horses win big races at 30-1 odds. But if you want a gamble to pay off, stick to the race track; that way, all you'll lose is money. Don't marry a long-shot.

However it is initiated, a good marriage is best entered by good friends. Some of the best marriages consist of couples who:

- were neither "madly in love" nor "crazy about each other";

- did not have "terrific chemistry";

- were not mirror images of each other's fantasies;

- represented matches made, not "in heaven," but right here on earth.

Since the real turn-on in a long-term relationship is intimacy, none of the above elements is necessary. And because these mythical standards are difficult to meet and virtually impossible to sustain, the inevitable letdown many couples encounter often interferes with the emergence of any real intimacy.

What is my definition of intimacy? Intimacy involves a trusting, caring, sharing, sensitive, and affectionate relationship—as well as a commitment to a partnership that makes allowances for imperfections. Sounds like love, doesn't it? Maybe so. But I've come across many couples who felt themselves to be in love while revealing few if any of the above characteristics. All of us know people who are sexually excited by someone they don't even like.

As I detail later on, love is very difficult to define, but a good working description, in terms of mature and immature relationships, is possible. This will give you an example of what I mean: the next time someone says to you, "I love you," and you don't really believe it, you might respond by saying, "Show me." Behavior counts more than words, however sincerely the words are intended. (And in this context, "show me" does not mean sex.)

Yes—I believe in love and sex. But love and sex are not enough to sustain a marriage. Falling in love certainly gets your attention. But friendship can (and does) outlast romance. Love comes and goes; friendship flows.

Sex and love (even a sweet, gentle love) *can* emerge in a marriage—once you've found a good friend to spend your life with. And it's even OK to decide to marry because you want a family, and to accept whatever uncertainty you have about love and sex. But keep your sense of perspective. Plan an exquisite wedding. Invite all your best friends and loved ones. Have a magnificent party. But don't be heartbroken if the two of you don't experience simultaneous orgasms on your wedding night.

If you're over 35 (regardless of your past marital status) it's probably best not to consider yourself constantly on the lookout for Mr. or Ms. Just Right. Your chances for a truly happy marriage are much better if you keep your eyes open for a *companionate* marriage—a marriage for friendship, rather than for the dream person you've been waiting for all your life. You may be surprised how readily love and intimacy grow within the open communication of genuine friendship. This friendship places a premium on enjoyable time together, trust, shared values, and a mutually compatible sense of humor.

In short, marry a good friend. Powerful love and sexual feeling can emerge in time, and will probably fluctuate somewhat. But the underlying friendship will serve as a strong foundation to the marriage. As the old blues refrain has it, love is like a faucet: it turns on and off. The intimacy of true friendship, on the other hand, continues to grow over the years.

Once one of your friends becomes a marital possibility, can you keep your other friendships? Certainly. One sign of a strong marriage is that it is expansive, and includes many opportunities for friendships, new and old. A weak marriage tends to be exclusive and limiting of outside relationships.

My friend Susan, who has been happily married for 35 years, was asked to give the secret of her success. She answered without hesitation: "I married him for better, for worse, for breakfast, and for dinner—but not for lunch." Unromantic? I don't think so at all.

Sexual attraction is something you may or may not feel at any given moment. It's a feeling, and remember that it is in the nature of feelings to change. While sexual attraction is notoriously unstable, authentic friendship is different. It has the capacity to sustain growth, as well as endure change. Friendship is more likely to feel better over time—and friendship's long-term potential can be tested more easily and reliably than that of attraction. Finally, friendship has the capacity to expand to include intimacy, which is, as we've noted, the true turn-on in a long-term relationship.

Intimacy and Shy People

According to studies reported by Jane Brody in the New York *Times* (November 16, 1989), 40% of adults describe themselves as shy. A significant number of these people are afraid that they will "make fools of themselves" by initiating contact with the opposite sex, and therefore will avoid making any overture at all. These fears are especially pronounced among insecure males, painfully aware of the fact that stereotype and custom often seem to dictate that men are "supposed to" make the first move.

Approaching shy people is one area where our assumptions about others are often unproductive, where offhand judgments (which everyone makes from time to time) can have unfortunate implications. Attractive people, for instance, often report that they suffer isolation—because they are deemed unapproachable by those around them.

If you're open to a relationship with a new person, try to avoid preconceived notions on this score. Intimacy, of course, has trouble flourishing if communication remains inadequate. When a woman encounters a reticent man, for instance, she should not dismiss him outright, but instead look a second time to see if there is a potential friendship. (Remember, friendship is the starting-point for any serious relationship.) Not every quiet or hesitant man acts the way he does out of a lack of interest in women, friendship, or sex. As a general rule, consider taking the initiative when you meet a person who seems reserved or withdrawn. Once the ice is broken, a shy person often becomes a fun-loving companion and a dependable friend.

While shyness may not be as obvious a handicap for a woman, it can often be the source of misunderstanding. Insecurity or silence is often read by men as aloofness (or even outright rejection)—and this can be devastating for the woman. A sensitive, gentle approach from a patient man can be a welcome relief to a painfully shy woman.

Dealing with shy people is one of the many areas of our lives where the great rewards go to the most observant.

Intimacy and Sex

Most modern Americans would be amazed to learn how many long-lasting, satisfying relationships got off the ground *without* great sex.

Intimacy and sex are *not* synonymous, and a strong relationship that is less than ideal sexually is not doomed. Good sex can be taught and learned, while the foundation of intimacy and trust on which a mature relationship is built must serve as a constant in the couple's mutual growth. In short, it is easier to develop good sex between good friends than it is to develop honesty and trust between great lovers.

Good sex does not occur spontaneously, and it takes place with somewhat less frequency than the bards of AM radio would have us believe. Simultaneous orgasm, while no fiction, is not common in the early stages of a sexual relationship—and it is not a prerequisite for mutually satisfying sex at any stage of a couple's time together.

Far from being any function of real intimacy and growth, sex today seems to be occurring more frequently with many partners who are enjoying it less. Currently, the more prevalent problem has to do with lack of sexual restraint, rather than lack of desire. (I suspect that in many good relationships, however, people are having sex less frequently and enjoying it more.)

I support rich, nurturing, fulfilling, energizing, illuminating, satisfying, enlightening relationships. But I am not an advocate of the quest for the perfect relationship. Such an idea is farcical, and the gurus who popularize these notions are fraudulent. Perfection (like the many other absolutes) exist nowhere in nature; some measure of happiness, trust, and intimacy within a real-life, flesh-and-blood relationship with an honest- to-goodness person is the goal.

Intimacy and Marriage

At what point has intimacy developed enough to allow a relationship to mature into a marriage?

Here are some basic guidelines. It is time to begin to consider marriage seriously when . . .

. . . the butterflies have passed.

. . . you are pretty sure your partner is not filling a gap in your life, but adding something precious to it.

. . . your love has stood the test of *some* time. After a year or so, you will know if your partner is caring, reliable, and trustworthy. You'll also be able to say with certainty whether your partner is involved in serious addictions (such as alcohol or gambling). Most important, you will know whether your partner is genuinely concerned about your welfare.

. . . you are content to accept this person with all his/her limitations.

. . . you believe that each of you is committed to the other's growth.

If you think the guidelines I've just set out don't have anything to do with *love*, I have to disagree. Let me list the characteristics of what I think love means—within a context of successful (that is, lasting and mutually satisfying) marriages that lead to strong families. The six traits are well known; they were first listed in the book *Secrets of Strong Families* by DeFrain and Stinnett, after a study of 6,000 married couples.

The six crucial traits of strong families are: mutual commitment (including time for children); significant time spent together; expressing appreciation of and for each other; spiritual wellness; the ability to face problems head-on and cope with them in positive ways; and open, honest communication.

In my view, these characteristics describe the true romance of marriage. Relationships that feature these traits open the way for sexuality and love to be interwoven with every aspect of life.

Examine your own heart; do you believe that the above can be true of you? Ask yourself: "How do I stack up as a potential marriage partner?"

Case History: A Marriage That Shouldn't Happen

Mary is impressed by Jason's BMW, and the fact that he looks and acts like the Yuppie he pretends to be. But he doesn't share much about his work life with Mary. Jason says things like, "Baby, when we get married, we're going to have four kids; you'll get to be a real housewife." Although Mary has more modern ideas about what she wants from her marriage, her expectations take a back seat to her desperation. After all, she is approaching the "unmarketable" age of thirty, and her parents like Jason a lot. For her part, Mary likes Jason's body more than she likes his character—he often comes across as ruthless, opinionated, and rigid. However, Jason is a Catholic, and Mary's parents are anxious to have a big church wedding. And all Mary's friends say that Jason is a great catch. So, despite her many unresolved doubts, Mary gives in. She puts all her energy into wedding arrangements and honeymoon plans, and is now almost finished deciding what she wants on her gift list.

Think Twice

Marriage is, optimally, a lifetime commitment. If there are significant doubts or unresolved problems in a relationship, the partners should resolve them *before* they walk down the aisle together—not simply trust that "things will work out."

After reading this book, you may decide, rightly and for perfectly valid reasons, that marriage is not for you. That's all right. There is no reason to feel guilty for making this decision; as your life changes, you are free to change your mind.

This book, however, is written mainly for those who want to marry, and who would like to maximize their chances of doing so successfully. In the next chapter, we'll learn how to take the first step.

Chapter Two:
Creating the New You

ARE YOU READY for a mature relationship?

The answer to that question depends, in large measure, on the answer to a great many other questions, the most important of which is: Are you a self-accepting person, or a self-defeating one?

Everyone has problems, to be sure. Each of us has areas of inadequacy. But the real question is, how do you approach the complex maze of attitudes, predispositions, thoughts, feelings, and past history that is you? Are you determined to put your best foot forward . . . or are you more likely to cheat yourself out of a positive outlook?

If you aren't sure who you are, if you don't feel good about that person, then you cannot expect someone else to do so. It's as simple as that. If you want to wind up in a challenging, mature, adult relationship—and certainly if you want to get married—you must have a pretty good idea of what can be expected from the person with whom your potential partner will be spending so much time.

Most of the ideas I will present here have been designed to help you achieve two main goals. The first is to help you establish strategies to develop, within yourself, a wholesome, non-narcissistic confidence in your identity. The second is to expand that self-knowledge into a mature, enriching relationship—the kind that must, eventually, deal with the unavoidable problems and challenges of real life. Immature love—either the egocentric kind we focus on ourselves, or the all-encompassing rush of passion and infatuation with which many relationships begin—is insufficient to sustain a long-term relationship. That's why this book is called *Why Love Is Not Enough*.

Some Danger Signs

Would you want to go out with yourself? If you called your house some evening and spoke with yourself, would you ask for a date?

Before you answer, think about the kind of image you present. Are you lonely or anxious? Are you worried that it is too late for you to "get" someone? Do you feel that the sooner you get married, the better off you'll be? Do you want to "find someone soon"? Are you, to put it bluntly, desperate?

If you want to stay that way, don't make any effort to change at all. Proceed with your usual methods. Take whatever hasn't worked (the singles bars, the classified ads, the uninspired and uninspiring blind dates) and keep trying—frantically. You may even want to try some new things that won't work: astrology, tarot cards, tea leaves, or renting billboard space to publicize your phone number.

Or you can accentuate the positive, beginning with the proposition that you are a good person. You can then proceed to address the question of your relationships with others by honestly asking yourself what you can do to become a better, happier individual. Someone you like.

Obviously, my advice is to consider the latter option. Take a personal inventory, see what it is you're presenting to the outside world in general and to potential partners specifically, and make some sober assessments. It may take some time, so if you are looking for instant solutions you may find the rest of this book unsatisfying.

There are no quick answers to the question of how best to initiate a satisfying, mature relationship.

Thankfully, though, the answers that are available will, if acted upon, probably make you a happier person.

How to Feel Better about Yourself

If you're still with me, and you agree that the second option is preferable to the first, here's my plan. It incorporates some concrete suggestions for making yourself more appealing by heightening your self-esteem.

Give up the meat markets. Entirely. No more singles bars, blind dates, or pickup discos. You should begin to view others as what they are—individuals—and not as conquests. By the same token, once you have determined that your objective is to enter a mature relationship, there is no reason for you to show up at these places. (Exceptions: singles nights sponsored by your church or synagogue or similar groups, or groups you attend to cultivate a new or passionate interest, such as book, travel, or nature clubs. Add to this list the thousands of other places people meet for reasons other than fleeting sexual encounters.)

Make a vow to take part in no casual sex. That means no sex with anyone who you feel has not made a commitment. Sound severe? Not really. If you are genuinely determined to wind up in a mature relationship, there's no longer any reason to put yourself in the no-win, short-term position of being someone else's "experience." Tennessee Williams once said that the reason so many women are willing to risk sex with anybody is because of the possibility of love. As his plays often reveal, the risk frequently does not pay off.

For many men, motivations underlying casual sex tend to incorporate another idea, called "scoring." What they fail to realize, however, is that their "scores" are often the very reason they find it difficult to develop long-standing relationships and/or successful marriages. They get a lot of practice making out and less practice making sense of their encounters.

In our society, people often use sex merely as a way to prove their masculinity or femininity, or as a tactic to *avoid* intimacy. (How's that for a paradox?) Consequently, many people— particularly single women—have found that sex with someone they don't really know often fulfills only the short-term partner's objectives. The very best way to gauge the strength and depth of any possible love relationship is to hold off having sex—whether you're male or female. Of course, there is the added incentive of preventing infertility or even death from a sexually transmitted disease, a potent argument against the one-night stand. I will discuss this issue in greater detail later in the book.

That's all very well, you may be saying to yourself, but just what am I supposed to do in the meantime? First, realize that sexual intercourse is not a physical requirement, and you are unlikely to develop psychological problems from not "getting enough." Second, accept that your feelings are genuine, understandable, and natural; do not feel guilty about wanting to go to bed with someone. Third, don't be afraid to masturbate. Age is no impediment here; if you need some creative ideas, read Betty Dodson's exceptional book, *Sex for One: The Joy of Selfloving* (Crown, 1987).

Tackle depression head-on. Let's face it; if you are reading this book, you're probably looking for a way to make your present, perhaps unsatisfying relationship more satisfying—or to find someone altogether new to fill what you may feel is a void in your life. If it's the first case, you get depressed from time to time. And, of course, if it's the second case, you also get depressed from time to time.

What do you usually do when you're depressed? (I'm referring here to "normal" depression that occurs as a result of unhappy times and experiences, not the kind that lasts for weeks and months regardless of circumstances, which requires medical care.)

Many people respond to depression by giving themselves permission to eat too much; or have a few too many drinks; or go on spending sprees; or gamble; or smoke a joint. Before you follow any of these paths, stop and try something new.

Go to the refrigerator. Find something sweet to eat and consume three or four non-compulsive mouthfuls. That will elevate your blood sugar and give you, without much difficulty, at least two "up" minutes.

Now use those two minutes to *learn something new*. Look up four new words in the dictionary. Go to that unread book you've had on the shelf for two years. Learn a magic trick. Select a brand new recipe to show off. Call up a friend and ask what's new—and if the response is "Oh, not much," hang up right away and call someone else.

Be unrelenting about learning something fresh and exciting during these two minutes. There is nothing more energizing than finding out something new, and there's virtually nothing more exhausting than being depressed. Use your renewed energy to continue on the path of fulfilling experiences.

Of course, it is perfectly OK to be depressed from time to time. Life is often full of disappointing developments, grief, and tragic happenings. But the message I hope I've gotten across here can go a long way toward helping you deal with such periods. That simple message is: Learning something new is an energizing, uplifting experience. Take advantage of that experience whenever you can.

Find an interest. Enhance your talents and skills in an area you have neglected to develop up to this point. Every person can profit from a passionate interest, an exciting hobby, and, last but not least, the opportunity to show off a creative talent.

There are a number of ways to accomplish this goal. Obviously, you can study—take a course at your local community college, for instance. Or you might join a special-interest, charitable, or community group that reflects something about which you have strong feelings. It could focus on any number of pursuits: environmental issues, public television, wildlife preservation, anti-nuclear advocacy, church- or synagogue-related activities; the list is practically endless.

Alternatively, you might set specific long-term goals for yourself and follow them up just as enthusiastically. You could learn a new language—and reward yourself by taking your next vacation to a foreign country where the language is spoken! Learn to play badminton. Take up a musical instrument. But whatever you do, take it seriously. Whatever you choose to do, take the time to do it well.

Do mitzvahs. What is a mitzvah? A biblical injunction to do good deeds. In contemporary usage, its practical definition would be something along the lines of "doing something good without expectation of any kind of compensation in return."

A mitzvah is *not* donating money to a charity and deducting the amount from your income tax return. A mitzvah is *not* something you remind someone of relentlessly after it's completed. A mitzvah is *not* being temporarily accommodating to friends or associates in the hope that they'll eventually like you and do favors for you.

Mitzvahs represent another potent weapon for tackling the problems of depression, unhappiness, and loneliness. Try it and see. Volunteer in a hospital; work with the homeless; become a Big Brother or Big Sister. (Call up your local United Way office or other volunteer center if you need more ideas.) In short, be helpful to someone who is more needy or vulnerable than you are.

If you are not ready for this because something terrible (such as the death of a loved one, or victimization in a violent crime) has taken place in your life, there are other options open to you. Join a support group that relates to your life experiences. Almost every city has dozens of such groups, and there's probably one that addresses your problem directly. In this way, you can be helpful to others who are in similar situations and still reap the benefits of "mitzvah therapy."

If that doesn't work, you might want to consider counseling as a valuable tool for examining your reaction to the difficult events in your life. Therapy will help you find out what's blocking your emotional progress or causing you to make the same mistakes repeatedly. For most run-of-the-mill-neurotics (i.e., just about all of us, excluding the mentally ill), it shouldn't take long to notice results. You should be able to see some progress in terms of your own insights within about ten sessions, as long as you work with a counselor or therapist whom you like and respect. (If you don't like and respect the therapist, find another. Therapists work for you, not the other way around.)

If you're not in shape, get yourself into shape. Schedule yourself for a full physical examination, and then make modest starts in the following areas.

Exercise regularly. Try to set up a workable plan with your doctor. At the very least, go for long walks regularly.

Control your weight. Reduce your sugar and red meat intake; make every effort to swear off fast food and deep-fried menu items.

Stop smoking. If you don't smoke, you will be happier, healthier, and more attractive to others. (And I know that quitting is easier said than done.)

Attend a health club. Joining a health club is an excellent way to formalize your commitment to the new you—and it's not a bad way to meet new people, either. (Be aware that the gymnasium is emerging as a new "meat market.")

Improve your personality. This may sound like too comprehensive a project or too vague a goal, but it is attainable.

You might start by dressing and looking as well as you possibly can. This will not only improve your standing with others but will also alter the way you feel about yourself.

Another good idea is to make a promise never again to say anything disparaging about yourself to anyone. Well, almost anyone. Reserve moderate self-criticism for the conversations you hold with your mirror or with your very closest friends. Self-deprecation is very boring. Even passing along the various injustices visited on you by the world at large should be an activity you share with people you know well and trust to hold your confidence. How interested are *you* when a co-worker moans about how he should be making more money at his age, or how hard it is for him to manage with prices so high?

Here's another tip: proceed from the central idea that you're a nice person. Even if you don't believe it, pretend. Or, as the old saying has it, "Fake it until you can make it." Start by saying "Thank you" loud and clear when you receive a compliment. The same "faking it" approach will work wonders when it comes to developing a sense of humor. If you have to, start by laughing when you hear others doing so. (Remember, the ability to laugh at oneself is one of the most important aspects of an attractive person.)

Along the same lines, you should be quite generous in your (legitimate and believable) compliments directed toward others. Feel free to say things like, "That's a nice shirt," "You look good today," or "What a lovely dress." As my mother used to say, "Zug a gut wort, es kost nit mehr." ("Say a good word, it doesn't cost more.") But be careful not to earn a reputation as an insincere person—don't go overboard.

Be optimistic even if it kills you. It won't. Far too many people, though, act as though it will. Often, being optimistic begins with the simple decision not to bring a negative attitude to the proceedings. For instance, avoid peppering yourself and your associates with the terms "have to," "got to," and "should have." These words carry negative, pessimistic, and judgmental connotations; they imply that you are unsatisfied with what has happened or with what is about to take place.

If you must undertake something you're not crazy about, do it with a smile. There's very little in life that doesn't present options of greater and lesser attractiveness. Make the best of the situations you encounter.

Improve your current relationships. Pay special attention to your relationships with parents and siblings. Try afresh to keep the lines of communication open with positive messages, but don't expect miracles after the first phone call.

Where family members are concerned, be especially polite. If things have been strained in the past, politeness will keep the relationship functioning and perhaps provide you with needed distance. Expressive love is wonderful, but if that is lacking in your family, begin with politeness; expressions of love may emerge gradually. If, after long and serious reflection, you truly believe that you can't make it with your parents, focus on new relationships.

Make it a point not to emulate your parents' undesirable traits with your own children (or nieces and nephews).

Be prepared to try forgiveness. One proven approach is to take the initiative, contact someone who has hurt you, and offer to bury the hatchet. Alternatively, you might ask forgiveness of at least one person whom you feel you have hurt in the past. This approach can yield surprisingly rapid results. The reason? Hostility, jealousy, and the desire for revenge all use up energy—energy you need for personal growth.

Remember the words of the famous American psychologist William James: "Wisdom is learning what to overlook." Perhaps some long-held grudge is standing in the way of your development and blocking healthy relationships with others.

Of course, you *will* have to stand up for some things; otherwise you'll be taken advantage of and run the risk of becoming trapped in victimizing situations. Try to strike a balance. In your relationships with family members and the world at large, try not to take everything seriously. The truth is, most of the things people get all worked up over matter very little. By all means, set your priorities and stick to them, but don't be afraid to forgive sometimes.

Concentrate on same-sex friends. In my experience, at any rate, people who cannot make friends of the same sex become poor marital partners. Cultivating same-sex friends is a good way to develop your capacity for long-term, mature relationships. When you can honestly say, "Someone like me thinks I'm a good person and enjoys my company," you'll eventually conclude that you are likable enough to be attractive to the opposite sex. (These dynamics are different in a homosexual relationship. Homosexuals in committed relationships often make excellent friendships with members of the opposite sex.)

When it comes to making new friends, take some risks. Unless you are willing to risk rejection, you are not likely to find acceptance. Mutual trust comes along the way, but not necessarily at the beginning. Without facing the initial risk, nothing happens.

It may help to bear in mind that failure is an event, not a person. As Eleanor Roosevelt put it, "No one can make you feel inferior without your consent." This is not a cheap, sentimental slogan, but an axiom that should stand as a first principle in how you look at your life.

Improve your intellect and broaden your horizons. Read a newspaper every day for at least 20 minutes. Read the New York *Times* on Sundays.

Watch public television regularly. Swear off junk television, or limit your intake to one mindless program per week. (You'll look forward to it more.) There is a lot of garbage on television. The more you watch it, the more bored you will become.

Try to read one self-help book a month. (Start with this one, of course.) You'll find recommended titles at the back of this book. Not included are the so-called "New Age" psychobabble books, which prescribe magic rather than rational action.

Some Complications

By now you are probably wondering, "How on earth am I going to get the time to do all these things?" The answer is: it may be tough. Try isolating one or two activities and doing them for twenty-one days. That way they'll become habits, ingrained parts of your life. Then you'll be free to move on to new challenges and, given time, you can address more of them. As the old nursery rhyme advises, "One thing at a time, and that done well, is a very good rule, as many can tell."

Remember that energy is mainly psychological, and that the process of *not* learning is exhausting. If you have nothing to look forward to after work, you'll be tired when you're finished working. Time and energy are easy to come by for those people who have a sense of purpose and dare to be optimistic. Their energy is often *generated*—not consumed—by pursuing meaningful goals. (And they hardly ever fuss about being too busy.)

The whole process will take some time. Certainly a number of months, and perhaps as long as a year. This raises an important question.

While you're busy developing the "new you," what do you do about all the people who are used to the "old you"? If you share activities and interests with certain friends or family members, and you suddenly find yourself altering those activities (perhaps because you feel they're impeding your growth), how do you deal with the inevitable pressure to go back to the "good old days"?

My advice is to be honest and, tactfully, let the other person in on the fact that the "good old days" didn't do you much good. Come right out and say that you're taking time to put your life in order. By acknowledging that you're looking for new strategies for self-fulfillment, you will be able to open yourself to criticism.

Accepting that criticism will require no small amount of tact and courage on your part, and you should know in advance that most of what others say *won't* be constructive. Keep an open mind.

And how about responding to people you just plain don't like? That's easy. Say as little as possible, don't get mad, and remember to smile a lot on your way to wherever it was you were going before you encountered them.

Patience

Be patient. Approach the task of making yourself happier and more confident by following the suggestions I have outlined in this chapter. You will eventually meet people you like.

Try, wherever possible, to do this in a "non-date" setting. Ask a friend to invite you and an "eligible" to a casual home dinner. Don't rush things. Meet first, consider the serious stuff later. (And remember, no one-night stands.)

Now is the time to be nice to yourself. Don't be afraid of what might happen. Take the risk. Start thinking of yourself as someone worth spending time with. Eventually, someone else will think of you in the same way.

Chapter Three:
Love—It Comes in
Two Varieties

LET'S TALK about love.

Love is difficult to define, much less to explain. Yet just about everyone would agree that a good relationship, and certainly a good marriage, should have a component of love in it. As a person who desires such a relationship, you hope that your partner will love you and that you will be able to love your partner, whether or not you feel that you have come to a full understanding of the meaning of the verb "to love."

Many of us get muddled when we start trying to nail down what love is. Part of the reason is, when it comes to love, people often feel so insecure about the matter that they don't know *what* they should expect. Often, the only guides provided by our culture are mass media stereotypes and over-romanticized visions of love we picked up during adolescence.

In addition, many of us come to the conclusion that being in love presupposes some degree of insanity. If you're really in love, the theory goes, you are by definition slightly paralyzed and more or less unable to function in the outside world. Is love really like that? And, if so, do we really want to be in it?

Looking at Love in a New Way

What is love? What's most important in a loving relationship? How can you tell if you're really in love?

Though love may be difficult to define, it is certainly an important part of virtually everyone's life. I believe that if you feel you are in love, then you are. But there is a catch: Though you may be in love with someone, it is incumbent upon you to ask what *kind* of love it is. The answer to that question can say a great deal about your relationship's long-term potential.

There are basically two kinds of love relationships: mature and immature. And neither term refers to age. The fact of advanced years is no guarantee of maturity. The sheer volume of failed second and third marriages should be enough to convince just about anyone that previous life experiences do not guarantee maturity on this score.

But what is mature love? The two types are relatively easy to distinguish. Admittedly, once you are in a "madly in love" situation, it is difficult to sort out anything. That is why it is important to think about these issues ahead of time.

Mature love is energizing; immature love is exhausting. In a mature love relationship, you find yourself full of energy, ready to tackle new challenges and push back the boundaries that define what is possible. As important as this energy is in the relationships of the young, it becomes even more essential in later life. (One of the nicest things about mature love is that, for older partners, it can offer serenity while still providing an important measure of vitality and excitement.)

Wonderful things happen when you're involved in a mature relationship. You genuinely enjoy your partner's company. You have time to do almost everything you want. You fulfill your responsibilities. You tend to get along well with family and friends. Occasionally, of course, you have arguments with your partner, but not often, as you naturally want to please each other.

All of this stands in marked contrast to what immature love delivers. You can supply the examples yourself, either from your life or someone else's. In this type of relationship, you're tired most of the time. You procrastinate more often. You tend to develop new problems at work. Your relationships with others—friends, siblings, parents—seem to require uncharacteristically constant fence-mending. Perhaps domestic responsibilities are more difficult for you to fulfill. ("Wash the dishes? Moi? I cannot do that! I am in love!")

In an immature love situation, you may even be involved in what's known as a "hostile-dependent" relationship, in which you can't stand being without the person you supposedly love so deeply, pine after him or her in the face of even short periods of time apart, yet fight and argue with your partner most of the time when you are together. Mood swings, accusations of jealousy, and (occasionally) even violent actions are the order of the day.

How You Treat Your Partner,
How Your Partner Treats You

Another clear difference between mature and immature love shows itself in the way the partners treat each other. People in mature love relationships tend to make an extra effort to be nice; people in immature love situations don't consider the implications of their remarks or actions and are often needlessly bitter, mean-spirited, or selfish.

Consider the following dialogues, the first representing an exchange in an immature relationship, and the second representing the same situation resolved more constructively in a mature love setting.

Paul: Honey, let's have sex.

Erica: I have a headache . . .

Paul: You have a headache. On my day off. You have a lot of nerve!

or . . .

John: Honey, let's have sex.

Robin: I have a headache. . .

John: I'm sorry you have a headache. I'll get you an aspirin. There's always tomorrow.

Security and Commitment to Mutual Growth

One of the most satisfying things about mature love is that it leads to a sense of security. This security comes from the knowledge that you've found a partner whom you can count on in an emergency, during illness, or when you're under a great deal of stress. There is genuine comfort in discovering someone with the capacity to share in both your dreams *and* your defeats. This is perhaps the most important characteristic of a stable, long- lasting partnership.

In a mature love relationship, partners aren't threatened by each other's success or achievements. Rather, they're committed to mutual growth and have a vested interest in the intellectual and emotional development of the other person.

Your partner may be a member of a study group that meets when you are busy, may visit a friend without you, or may develop an interest in which you are unable or unwilling to participate. By the same token, you may want to take a course that helps you develop a favorite hobby, set up a work or volunteering schedule that doesn't include your lover, or simply meet a friend at a favorite cafe. None of these developments will be threatening, because mature people are proud of each other's interests and achievements. They realize that, in the long run, these things indirectly benefit both parties by encouraging a challenging, rewarding marriage.

The immature relationship, however, is usually characterized by insecurity, tension, impetuousness, uncertainty, frequent fights, frequent make-ups, and impressive measures of lust and infatuation. If one person achieves something significant, the other may easily feel threatened and become depressed.

People in immature relationships may often find themselves peppered with questions such as: "Do you love me?" "Do you *really* love me?" "Do you love me more than you love (name of a former lover)?" (When such queries are a constant component of the relationship, my advice is to answer "no" and see what happens. Doing so will almost certainly do one or more of three things: get a more interesting conversation going; shock the questioner into looking at him or herself; or encourage more honest discussion about the relationship.)

Promises, Promises

Does any of this sound familiar?

"Don't worry, honey, when we get married, I'll stop fooling around. You know you're the only one for me."

"I'm never going to get drunk again. I swear it. I've learned my lesson."

(Two months later:) "I'm never going to get drunk again. I swear it. I've learned my lesson."

"Please don't leave. I promise I'll stop gambling, just don't go away."

Immature love is full of promises. When the promises cover up personal problems or habitual self-destructive behavior, there can be trouble. When the promises form the basis of a decision either to continue a relationship or to make a lifetime commitment, difficulties are sure to surface.

Bad situations are *always* made worse by marriage. Certainly people do change, and personal habits can be turned around. But when you have heard the same excuse several times, with no noticeable change in your partner's behavior, it is time to take a good long look at the relationship.

Mature love seems to depend far less than immature love on promises to atone and pleas for belief in a partner's turning over a new leaf. Mature lovers know each other, and don't require constant reassurance of a partner's newfound virtue. When there are challenges to the relationship—as there inevitably are—each side examines the problem as a knowledgeable participant in the ongoing process of building a life together, and not as a salesperson approaching a wary customer who, with a little different pitch, may eventually be persuaded to purchase a questionable product.

Is It Infatuation?

Let's assume that you are in the beginning stages of a relationship. How will you be able to tell whether it is immature and based on infatuation, or a potential mature love that deserves (and can support) a commitment?

During the first weeks of the relationship, the two types may be virtually indistinguishable. But after the intense preliminary period (which may last as long as a month, or perhaps longer in the summertime), some differences will emerge.

If it is infatuation, the couple's intense feeling will begin to go sour, and some bitterness may emerge. As you get to know each other better, the other person may no longer seem as sensitive, appealing, or easy to talk to. For at least one of the partners, love begins to feel like something of a burden.

Even in cases where couples are still madly in love, people in immature relationships tend, more and more, not to care what the other person thinks about them. (Indeed, many wind up unconcerned about what *anyone* thinks about them.) They may neglect their studies or their work; they may be careless about their appearance; they may quickly become jealous, irritable, or petty; they may neglect important responsibilities.

In a relationship that has the potential for mature love, however, the process of becoming better acquainted with each other continues to be enjoyable and exciting. The more you get to know the other person, the more you find to like and admire. You are inspired to take extra pains with work or studies; to groom yourself carefully and look as appealing as possible for your partner; or simply to put forth the best aspects of your personality.

What Some People Say About Love, and What You Could Say In Response

If you loved me, you'd sleep with me. If you loved me, you wouldn't make demands like that. (Sex is never a test or proof of love, and you cannot buy love with sex. Unfortunately, it's still true that many women have sex because of the possibility of love, while many men have sex because of the possibilities of sex. Remember that sex is frequently confused with love, and that there are happy couples who love each other a great deal with what some might consider inadequate sex lives.)

If you have sex before marriage, you'll have nothing to look forward to and all the surprise will be removed from your relationship. If sex is the only surprise in marriage, then no one should get married. (Frankly, sex alone is not worth it.)

Love is blind. Only for twenty-four hours. Then you have to open your eyes.

Stand by your man (or woman). Sure, but stand up for yourself, too. If someone forces sex on you, consistently makes unreasonable demands, or beats you up, that has nothing to do with love, no matter what anyone says. There are more likely explanations for such behavior: insensitivity, neurosis, dependency, or fear.

You really fall in love only once in a lifetime. Nonsense! Though a good argument can be made against the possibility of being genuinely in love with more than one person at a time, even the most intense love affair may be followed by another relationship that stands or falls on its own merits. That relationship may be even more deeply rooted and emotionally satisfying than the one preceding it. Along the same lines, bear in mind that your world does not end when a relationship ends. Mature love is a shared experience; when someone does not return your affections, do your best to deal with the pain of natural disappointment, but accept the possibility that other relationships may be more rewarding.

Keep a stopwatch on your partner and get every bit of time from him or her that you have coming. It's the only way you can really feel good about yourself or your relationship. Requiring constant attention and "T.L.C." is not the mark of a mature relationship.

Love comes only to the "beautiful people." Mature love is not determined by looks, income level, or social status. People who have some measure of self-esteem are attractive to some other people. Period. Everyone is unique. Everyone's life can be enriched by love. Do not ask the cosmetic and toiletries manufacturers what they have to say about this; they have a vested interest in selling perfume, hair tonic, vaginal spray and wrinkle cream to make your life "better," so they lie. (Have you ever noticed how few "cover girl-to-playboy," made-in-heaven match-ups pass the test of time?)

The Signs of a Mature Love Relationship

Erich Fromm, in his classic *The Art of Loving*, describes four criteria that characterize a mature love relationship. According to Fromm, in such a relationship both partners care for each other, respect each other, assume responsibility for each other, and develop joint understanding.

Another good yardstick is put forward by Robert J. Sternberg, professor of psychology at Yale University. Dr. Sternberg believes that the three most crucial ingredients in a successful relationship are commitment, intimacy, and passion.

Finally, we come to my list. My items are more pragmatic than the two I have mentioned, though obviously you are encouraged to use all three lists in evaluating your relationships. Love is an inexact science. You will probably have your own standards. Use the list below as a starting point, not as the last word.

I should say that in any relationship, commitment is imperative. That element is so important that it underlies the entire list, yet it is not spelled out here. If commitment does not exist, there is no point in making up a list in the first place.

That having been said, here is my list of the ten most important characteristics of a mature relationship.

One: Intimacy. Closeness, trust, and the ability to sustain a caring, loving relationship through good times and bad.

Two: A sense of humor. Willingness to laugh at oneself and the world at large. (If it is extremely difficult for you to develop a sense of humor, please do not plan on raising a family; laughter is a compulsory skill when it comes to bringing up children.)

Three: Honest communication. Openness and good listening skills.

Four: A common sense of mission and purpose. Shared ethical and/or spiritual goals.

Five: Equality. A conscious sense of the essential importance of respect for each other as partners, and shared responsibility in career, leisure, child rearing, and lifestyle choices.

Six: A sense of adventure. A desire to keep the relationship fresh; new and interesting ways of expressing affection for each other.

Seven: Shared experience. An ever-growing repository of mutual undertakings, private conversations, and shared thoughts on issues and events, as well as celebrations, rituals, and traditions you both enjoy.

Eight: Respect for the other person's feelings and wishes. The willingness to delay one's own short-term desires in the knowledge that a similar willingness will exist on the part of the other person at a later time; specifically, respect for the partner's feelings toward sex in any given instance.

Nine: Passion. Including, but not limited to, a healthy sex life.

Ten: Sharing in domestic duties. Not being limited by gender stereotypes; not allowing one partner to claim a monopoly on all household tasks for the purpose of taking on a martyr role. Accepting responsibility for doing one's fair share of the more unpleasant household tasks.

As I indicated earlier, the rankings are to some degree matters of individual taste and perception. Nevertheless, anything that makes it into the "top ten" is, by definition, of major significance in a relationship. I'd recommend thinking seriously and creatively about how and where the above guidelines can be incorporated into your life with your partner.

I have been chided, in the past, for not including financial security on the above list. There are many successful relationships, however, that thrive in adverse financial circumstances. In my view, justification for including this item on the indispensable list simply doesn't exist. Then again, it could be reasonably considered to be a strong candidate for number eleven on an extended list.

Of related interest, *Self* magazine polled 1,000 women in 1989 and found that they rated sex fifth in importance in a marriage, behind communication, appreciation, companionship, and being able to share in child-care and chores.

"Madly in Love"

For one neurotic reason or another, men and women sometimes fall hopelessly in love with people they don't even know very well, let alone like. Sometimes it becomes an obsession; nothing else on earth seems to matter except that one person. Like any other addiction, such an obsession can (and often does) become very destructive for all concerned. Sometimes people will fall madly in love with those who not only don't return the affection, but are outright hostile as well.

If there's no rational component to a love relationship, the odds are against its surviving over time. In addition, it's not uncommon to find that "madly in love" has become "tragically in love." More often than not, the love object is a fantasy. When the real person emerges, the disappointment and bitterness can be quite severe, sometimes even violent.

On the other hand, people sometimes *back away* from relationships with others whom they like and respect, not simply as a result of a fear of commitment (the currently fashionable diagnosis for all such problems), but too often because they don't feel the intense passion, heat, or reckless abandon of "mad" love. (This very often occurs after a failed relationship or marriage that began "madly.")

In any case, my advice is to get acquainted with each other first, then decide if there is the potential for a serious relationship.

Changes

Needless to say, some relationships may start out immaturely and mature later on. All relationships begin (and continue to grow) with elements of immaturity. That is why all marriages incorporate a certain amount of tension at any given moment. Marriages are about growth, and the very idea of growth necessitates a passage from a lesser degree of maturity to a greater one.

Still, the relationships that are the most durable usually have mutual commitment as their central and strongest component. Though every marriage will undergo changes in levels of intimacy, passion, and communication, if there is commitment, that relationship has possibilities.

That there is always some level of immaturity present in any relationship means that, for each partner, there is a certain amount of risk. Leo Buscaglia argues again and again that those who want to love truly have no choice but simply to do so, without guarantee of reciprocation; they have no choice but to believe, accept, and trust . . .

and hope that the love they give others will be returned. No guarantees. No assurances. Just the decision to love.

And that is the paradox. Even the mature relationship has at its heart a certain instability. Such a relationship does not incorporate a mechanical, 50-50 division of emotional support, material contribution, or decision-making power and ability. Mature love creates its own balance, with the partnership progressing through ever-changing, ever-challenging phases. One party may be in a dominant position in one area for a time, only to be followed by the other partner's ascension a little later. Love, like life itself, is a changing, fluid proposition. It cannot be negotiated finally or reduced to a fixed set of equations. It must be born, live, and thrive in a changing world.

Chapter Four:
Before You Say, "I Do . . ."

YOU HAVE DECIDED that you've entered a mature love relationship. You may even want to get married. (I hope you agree with me that there is no reason to marry unless the relationship is mature.) You are willing and able to take the plunge. Now is the time to stop and think.

These days, many (if not most) marriages are unsuccessful. About half of all recent marriages break up within ten years. The Census Bureau has estimated that of all American women who have ever been married, 24 percent have had at least one divorce. The estimated figure for men is much higher. About 40 percent of all U.S. marriages in the 1980s were remarriages. To be sure, the figures are sobering.

This is not meant to frighten you away from marriage. The high divorce rate does not guarantee that your marriage will be unsuccessful; you should not bow in fear to the odds that you will end up divorced if your parents divorced. In life, nothing is inevitable but death.

Specifically, do not count yourself out if you are a woman over the age of thirty who is looking for a serious relationship. As the media trumpets regularly, there are statistically fewer single men available in this age group than you might like, but do you really want to let your self-image, your love life, and your future be determined by marginal statistics? You are a person, not a number. Your life is determined by what you put into it; the demographics may incline, but they cannot compel. (It is interesting to note that many of the early and overpublicized "scare studies" in this area were statistically flawed, since they failed to take into account the number of men who become available each year as a result of divorce.)*

Statistics do not get married—people do. There are still a lot of real-life examples of good marriages, even among couples with two sets of divorced parents, family histories of alcoholism, or any other negative profile you care to name.

My purpose here is to tell you why many contemporary marriages are not successful, in the hope that this knowledge might help you reflect on your own decision to marry a particular person and perhaps reevaluate that decision, where you feel it is appropriate to do so.

Wrong Turns

Of course, there are many reasons marriages do not succeed. Couples marry for any number of wrong reasons.

---

* The good news on this front for women is that recent research indicates the year 1987 was something of a turning point demographically. The overall pool of men (from which single men are drawn) has grown relative to the overall pool of women. Based on estimates from the U.S. Census Bureau, the New York Times (January 17, 1990) reported that single men in their 20s outnumber single women of the same age by more than a 6-5 ratio. In fact, there are some 2.3 million more unmarried men than women in this group. It is of more than passing interest that of the two million weddings each year, 22 percent (approximately 440,000) are now between women and younger men. There's another significant statistic: In 1990, four in ten American adults were single.

The least rational motive for wanting to spend your life with someone is sex; this overemphasis on sex constitutes a major reason for marital failure.

You can be sexually attracted to someone with whom you cannot even hold a conversation. You can have an affair with someone you would not consider an appropriate parent. You can be sexually excited by *parts* of people. But you cannot expect to build a lasting, satisfying relationship with someone with whom you share only sexual interests.

The next irrational reason is, surprisingly, love. Being in love is not an adequate reason to marry. Let me reemphasize: Love alone is no excuse for marriage. People who marry only or mainly for love (because they're "crazy about each other," believe they have "a marriage made in heaven," think they are "meant for each other," or are convinced it was "love at first sight"), very seldom have successful marriages and more often than not separate or divorce.

Many people are shocked when I say this. Although it is perfectly natural and desirable to be sexually attracted and in love with the person you marry, marriage is meant to be an intellectual and rational decision; you could be madly in love with someone who is totally unacceptable as a marital partner. (Experienced marriage counselors can confirm this with innumerable examples.)

In marriage, the issue is not how much you are in love—or even how compatible you are, or what common interests you share. The real issue is, how are you going to deal with the inevitable incompatibilities that are part and parcel of any marriage?

Consider the following scenarios. Each represents a real situation in which the apple of someone's eye turned out to be "someone else entirely" within only a few months of the wedding.

The strong, silent, romantic man you married has suddenly become morose and anxious after losing his "secure" job (or after the birth of the first baby, or after being forgiven for a discovered affair).

Your charming, loving, witty, and independent girlfriend has become a dependent, overly solicitous, complacent wife.

Her independence was what attracted you most. Now that it's gone, she is driving you nuts, and you feel that your marriage is becoming boring.

The gracious, fun-loving, intellectual, nonsexist young man you married is now, after five years of marriage, a workaholic first and foremost. Even though you work full time too, he seems angry and tired most of the time, and will no longer participate in household tasks—let alone spend time with the kids. ("It's the wife's job," he says, using words that would never have passed his lips a few years back.) When you call the changes to his attention, his response is: "You're lucky I don't gamble or drink like Johnson down the street does. Don't I bring home my pay every week? And I'm not having an affair. I work hard to give you and the family a good standard of living, and all you do is nag and fuss. I'm fed up!" Is this the person you were so crazy about just a few years ago?

What happened? From all indications these couples were in love, once upon a time. Yet each marriage is lost. Each couple would have benefited greatly from a premarriage decision to take the time and energy to sort out some of the issues, questions, conflicts, and problems that eventually surface during just about any marriage. (For some of the issues and problems you should discuss with each other, please see chapter five.) And yes, you can (and should) begin this process before you walk down the aisle.

"I" Messages

Before asking the questions and discussing the issues with your partner, however, you need to develop an effective way of communicating. This is not related to how much is said; some people are natural talkers; some are silent types. Silence can mean passive-aggressiveness or indifference, but it can also be a thoughtful response.

An effective communication model is perhaps the most important element in developing a secure and lasting marriage—and good communication begins with using "I" messages. Here are some examples illustrating the difference between harmful communication (using "you" messages) and good communication (using noncombative, nonthreatening "I" messages).

Instead of telling your partner:

> If I've told you once, I've told you a hundred times: you should be on time when we're meeting someone for dinner.

Try saying:

> It's really embarrassing to me when I have to make excuses for you not arriving for dinner on time. I know you don't do it deliberately. Would you like me to call you at the office to remind you? I'd really appreciate your cooperation.

Instead of saying:

> If you really loved me, you would remember to take out the garbage.

Try saying:

> It upsets me when I have to remind you to take the garbage out. I know, it is a dumb thing to fuss about, especially since you agreed it was your job, but do you think we could work out a solution? Should I leave you a note or . . .

Instead of complaining:

> If you cared for me, you wouldn't go fishing with your buddies.

Try saying:

> I know how much you enjoy your fishing trips, but with my schedule, the weekends are the only time we get to spend time together. Is there some compromise I can work out with you?

Instead of saying:

> If you really loved me, you wouldn't go on about the trouble you're having at work when I get home exhausted from my job.

Try saying:

> Honey, I know your job is difficult. I want to talk about it, but I find I can't be very helpful when we discuss it when I've just gotten home. I'd really appreciate it if we could set another time to talk.

Instead of verbally attacking your partner, saying:

> If you had even the least bit of consideration for me you wouldn't hang out with that silly friend of yours, Leslie. You know I can't stand Leslie.

Say:

> Darling, I realize that we have different opinions about some of our friends. I'd be more comfortable, if I didn't hear about the time you spend with Leslie.

If your partner says, "You seem upset," instead of replying:

> No, I'm not. Why do you always want to start arguments?

Say:

> I guess there must be something wrong, because I'm not feeling upset. What do you think is happening?

In each of the examples, the latter example represents the positive communication patterns that emerge in healthy relationships. Start using this method now with friends, lovers, and parents. Again, it isn't anything fancy—but it can make all the difference in assessing your relationship's potential. Using "I" messages may not be easy to at first, but communicating in this way is one of the best preparations for a successful marriage. "I" messages encourage the art of compromise and represent the best way to avoid speaking in attacking, hurtful, blaming ways. Here are a few guidelines to keep in mind.

Avoid statements such as:

You'll never amount to anything

You're just plain rotten

You hate me/I hate you

You always/never

Why? These statements—and all of their possible variations—tend to polarize your conversation, and, by extension, your relationship. They leave your partner with little or no room to respond maturely, as an equal. Once you find a more accessible way to state the same points you feel strongly about, you'll be on the way to a better level of communication. No one is suggesting that you repress anger—but you should express your anger in a constructive manner, resolve it, and use it to fuel change. Unexpressed anger will submerge, fester, and resurface disguised as a symptom such as depression or alcoholism, or as physical illness or physical violence.

The sooner you learn how to negotiate your relationship's (inevitable) conflicts, the better off you'll be. Whether you like it or not, there will be fights in marriage; this should not worry anyone.

George Bach, author of *The Intimate Enemy*, sees occasional, intense, angry exchanges as indications of genuine involvement and caring. The trick is to learn how to fight in a nonhurtful way. Messages filled with venomous asides and ominous threats are the first danger signs in a disintegrating relationship.

Here are some of Dr. Bach's rules for fair fighting:

State a specific source of dissatisfaction, without sitting in judgment of the person's whole character.

Do not betray a partner's trust by bringing up the vulnerabilities he or she has shared with you.

When a person passes on a gripe, feed it back to him/her as accurately as possible. This encourages listening, rather than waiting for one's turn to talk.

Do not make assumptions about the other person's thoughts, feelings, or motives. (Remember the old saying about how assume makes an ass out of u and me?)

Do not correct a partner's statement about his or her feelings. What he or she feels is his or her reality.

Don't complain for the sake of complaining. Ask for a reasonable change that will relieve the gripe.

Never put restrictive, limiting labels on a partner: child, drunk, workaholic, slut, neurotic, male chauvinist pig.

I might add that once you do get involved in an argument, saying "It's all my fault" won't resolve anything any more than saying "It's all your fault" will. Similarly, saying "I'm sorry you feel this way" is much better than saying "You must be dense not to get what I'm saying."

"I" messages and fair fights are good things to explore before marriage. But suppose it is after you are married that you fall into the pattern of making hateful statements and fighting unfairly? Suppose you feel you are drifting toward a breakup?

Rule Number One is, talk to each other. If that doesn't work out, try marriage counseling or a marriage encounter group. Don't assume the problem will go away. There is no substitute for finding out what troubles one partner about the other.

Try experimenting with a few changes. Agree that you will or won't do this or that for a month, without complaining; see how it goes. Also, experiment with a radical technique called being nice to each other—even if it's superficial. It might sound like this:

Honey, is there anything that I can get for you?

No, thanks, dear; I'm fine.

At first, it may seem forced. But stick with it. You'd be surprised what a couple of months of old-fashioned politeness can do for a troubled relationship. See what happens when you follow the old rule about not saying anything at all when you can't say something nice.

This approach may sound phony to you now, but it isn't at all. It will give you the breathing space and energy to consider whether a troubled marriage is worth fighting for.

You might still be afraid to take another chance or even make the commitment to the marriage that has been lacking all along. Do remember, however, that until you're willing to risk getting hurt, there's no point in even trying to make the commitment. Every meaningful interaction involves risk.

Of course, there are many more reasons behind failed marriages, including money problems, the birth of a handicapped child, interfering in-laws, marrying too young, or resentment of the spouse over an early problem in the relationship (such as an unwanted pregnancy that "forced" marriage). However, the basic communication rules apply. Learn them before you get married, or failing that, learn them now.

Broadly speaking, what kinds of women bother men most? Those who are unfaithful, abusive, self-centered, condescending, sexually withholding, neglectful, and moody. What kinds of men bother women most? Those who are sexually aggressive, unfaithful, abusive, condescending, emotionally constricted, neglectful of their appearance, or too openly admiring of other women. (Source: Daniel Golemen's article in the New York *Times*, June 13, 1989.) Considering how prominent infidelity is in those two lists, you may be wondering why I have not mentioned the affair as a factor in marital breakup. In my experience, an affair is a symptom of a marriage that is already troubled. In fact, an affair by itself rarely breaks up a marriage, and can sometimes initiate new attempts at communication. What the crisis of a revealed affair does is give the couple an opportunity to decide whether to try again or to call it quits and get a divorce.

Compromises, Commitments

We have looked, so far, at the various reasons marriages break up. To conclude this chapter, though, let's look at some positive aspects. It's at least as important to do this as it is to forecast the risks. After all, you don't want a relationship that "doesn't fail," you want one that succeeds in challenging and enriching both partners.

What should a good marriage have?

We'll address the question in detail later in the book, but a few comments are appropriate here. Good marriages invariably involve compromise. The passionate, all-encompassing period of attraction in marriage usually lasts only a few months. Unrealistic expectations and media-inspired notions of marriage eventually dissolve with the predictable, daily advance of real life. In a relationship begun with unrealistic expectations, disappointment sets in quickly.

What keeps the best marriages going is commitment to the other person in the relationship. Once a rational decision to marry has been made, commitment becomes the key issue.

No marriage really works unless each partner is committed to the other's growth—and unless, as M. Scott Peck suggests in his excellent book, *The Road Less Traveled*, "a person makes a commitment to be loving whether or not a reciprocal loving feeling is present. In effect, this commitment says, 'Yes, there will be anger and fights. And yes, we'll try to work out a system of resolving arguments. I will stay with you. I'll be patient, and I will love you even when you are not lovable. I hope you will do the same for me.' "

Eventually, any serious relationship must involve reciprocity, but that isn't enough. Patience, too, is required for those times when your partner's concern and caring aren't as obvious as you might wish.

Chapter Five:
One on One—Questions, Issues, and Problems

MANY COUPLES DAYDREAM a great deal about all the wonderful things they'd like to see happen once they get married. There is nothing wrong with that. It is normal and certainly enjoyable. But, in addition to daydreaming, I urge you to consider real-life questions, and to imagine some real-life situations.

Take the time and energy to sort out, with your partner, as many of the relationship's potential conflicts, issues, questions, and problems as possible, before either partner builds up unrealistic expectations or creates unreasonable demands. In this chapter, we will try to examine what sort of questions you should be asking your partner, once you feel confident that you have entered into a mature relationship—one you could reasonably expect to see grow into something special.

The very act of composing a list of "questions one should ask" is something of an exercise in optimism. After all, no two relationships are alike, and no one can anticipate all of the potential challenges and decisions a couple will face. Nevertheless, it is essential to make the effort. If you do not pose the applicable what-if questions (and you should certainly feel free to add your own questions to my list), you may be rudely awakened later on in your relationship when you and your partner disagree violently over something that should have been discussed before you decided to marry.

Marriage

While the main thrust of this book is to address the challenge facing anyone who attempts to build a lasting love relationship, the questions I pose in this chapter are, for the most part, of greatest relevance to couples who are seriously considering getting married. With that in mind, it is probably time to discuss the institution of marriage.

There are, of course, many different kinds of marriage. There are marriages of convenience, which feature little long-term passion or intimacy; there are marriages of desperation, in which at least one and probably both partners have significant self-esteem problems; there are old-fashioned marriages, with rigidly defined gender roles; and there are what I call the best-case marriages, those offering an exciting balance of intimacy, passion, and commitment.

My suggestions in this chapter are directed toward those couples in a mature relationship who feel that the last option is the one they choose to pursue as a marital objective. (I should note, too, that this chapter is also pertinent for people who have what I've described earlier as a companionate relationship: one that could develop into a best-case marriage.) My questions make the assumption that the relationship is more or less egalitarian in conception, if not always in practice.

Let me explain what I mean. An egalitarian relationship does not require that the wife be discouraged from staying at home and taking care of the children, or pressured into finding a "real job." (Child care—including its associated domestic duties—is easily equivalent to at least one full-time job and probably more, as anyone who's tried it will tell you.) Furthermore, an egalitarian relationship does not demand that the man automatically forego the role of breadwinner, nor does it dictate that a woman can't cook and prepare all the meals if this arrangement is based upon mutual agreement. What an egalitarian relationship does demand is a commitment to equal opportunities in decision making, specifically including choices related to career, child rearing, and lifestyle questions.

It is in this context that the strongest marriages address important issues, and it is to couples who want to build such marriages that the following points are addressed.

The Questions

Before you ask your partner any of the following questions, consider discussing the topics of honesty and risk-taking in your relationship. Many of the issues addressed below are considered sensitive by some people, and if your partner is prepared for this, you are more likely to have a productive discussion.

Careers

If both couples work, does it matter who earns the most?

If both couples work, what if one of us is offered a new job at significantly higher levels of pay and responsibility—in a different part of the country? What is my reaction if it's you?

What if one of us wants to pursue further education or get a higher degree?

What if one of us wants to start a new business?

What about retirement plans?

Family

Do we want children? If so, when and how many?

Will we share equally in caring for the baby, including diaper changes?

Does either of us have strong ideas about how a child should or should not be raised? If so, what are they? If not, how should we address the issue?

Finances

Will we have separate or joint bank accounts?

Will we need life insurance? If so, how much?

Is a prenuptial agreement appropriate? How do you feel about such agreements?

Should we save as much of our income as we can or try to live as well as possible on what we make now? If we decide to save, what is worth saving for?

What do you think about borrowing money? Credit? Credit cards?

Assuming that we have the choice on a purchase of a major appliance (say, a refrigerator) should we give most serious consideration to a top-of-the-line model or something on sale? Why?

Of the two of us, who is the bigger spender? How does the other partner feel about this?

Is it important to either of us to purchase an item primarily because a neighbor or other acquaintance has a similar item?

Living Arrangements

Where will we live once we get married?

Does either of us have strong feelings about furniture, design, or floor plans in our living space?

How will we allocate household tasks? Does either of us have strong likes or dislikes about particular tasks?

How do we usually handle disagreements?

How much of our past have we shared with each other up to this point? Is it necessary to share everything?

With whose parents do we anticipate spending most of our in-law time, such as holidays and family gatherings? Will we attempt to split this time? How will we handle any problems that may arise in this area? Does either of us feel we must kowtow to future in-laws? Why? What happens if we tire of doing so?*

What level of support do our parents anticipate for their old age?

How important is religion in our life together?

Do we have to be together all the time? Can we have separate interests? What about occasional separate vacations?

In addition to our mutual acquaintances, can we have friends whom the other partner does not know or spend time with? What if one of us has a friend the other genuinely dislikes?

How do we feel about pets? Does either of us have strong negative reactions or allergies to certain animals?

---

*If in-laws try to interfere or unduly influence your marriage, it's best to work out some kind of specific compromise with your spouse. You might reach an agreement along the following lines: "We'll go to your folks' place for Thanksgiving and I'll listen to their harangues politely, but without commitments to change things about which I simply disagree. On Christmas Day, we'll go to my folks' house, and then you can play sweetness and light without having to pay attention to any of the snide remarks they make about your cooking." Again, it's OK under certain circumstances to fake it!

How should we spend our leisure time together? Are we willing to compromise on this issue if there is a disagreement?

If either of us does something the other person doesn't like, can we

a) agree not to confront each other about it in public, and discuss it in an appropriate private setting?

b) address the issue in a polite manner?

c) listen to the other person's reaction to the criticism objectively?

Personal (Advanced Level)

Assume that one of us finds someone else attractive, appealing, or interesting. Is it all right to say so? Or would you prefer that I kept such thoughts to myself? Would I prefer that you do the same?

How would either of us feel if there were some irritating character traits or behaviors that the other person was unwilling or unable to change?

Are there things either of us finds unappealing about the other person? What have we avoided saying to keep from hurting the other person's feelings? Are there "ticking time-bombs" that may eventually explode in any of the following areas?

Quirks

Poor hygiene or bad breath

Little or no sense of humor

Personal mannerisms

Clothes selection or general appearance

Behavior in front of in-laws or friends

Compulsive behavior

Suppose one of us is infertile and we cannot have children together. Would we remain childless? Divorce? Adopt a child? If adoption is our response, do we have any preconditions (for instance, that the child be of a certain race or sex)? How far would we be willing to pursue the other fertility options?

Suppose (God forbid) we have a child who is born severely handicapped. How would we respond? What would the implications of caring for such a child be in relation to our other life objectives?

If one of us wants something from the relationship and doesn't get it, can the topic be raised diplomatically, and not in a confrontational manner? If the other partner feels as though he or she is being attacked in such situations, how will we keep communication open?

In order to make a realistic compromise, how willing are we to give up something pleasurable that may annoy the other person?

If one of us is not in the mood to have sex when the other partner suggests it, will we be able to remember that we still both care about and love each other?

What do we hope our life together will be like five years from now? ten years from now? 20 years from now? 50 years from now?

(Regardless of age:) When I grow up, I'd like to be a _____. What would you like to be when you grow up?

What do you least like about yourself? What do I least like about myself? Can we work out a system that will allow each of us to discreetly tell the other person when he or she is engaging in activities that need improvement?

We feel good about the relationship now, but what if one of us, someday, feels the urge to have an affair? What is the difference between fantasizing about an affair and actually engaging in one? What about flirting with others—do we consider it harmless? If one of us were to genuinely desire to have an affair, are our communication skills strong enough to discuss a potential crisis openly? Would we see a marriage counselor? Most importantly, do we trust each other not to let the marriage disintegrate by perpetuating a dishonest approach to our relationship?

Of course, over the years, there are hundreds of other issues that will arise in a marriage. But the points addressed above represent a healthy start in sorting out problems and potential trouble spots. Asking (and honestly answering) questions like the ones posed in this chapter will strengthen your relationship and encourage both partners to develop mature communication skills.

Men and Women, Women and Men

Issues like the ones I have outlined here are important to address before marriage. It is potentially disastrous to learn, after the honeymoon, that one's spouse has rigid expectations that were misinterpreted (or simply not discussed) early in the relationship.

Many of the most common misunderstandings are gender-based. Research into the causes of modern marriage problems has consistently shown that there are significant differences in the ways men and women are socialized to accept marital roles. No matter how strongly you feel about your relationship, you should know about these general tendencies on the part of each sex before you get married.

For instance, most women tend to view intimacy as a shared commitment to address important issues and problems—as a couple. Men, by contrast, feel they've fulfilled their obligations once they've done their share (e.g., performed specific, predetermined chores; brought home a paycheck according to schedule; or taken the next turn putting the children to bed). Does this dynamic seem to reflect developing patterns in your relationship?

Another point of departure: conflict resolution. While women typically view the discussion of differences as a way to get closer to their partners, conventional wisdom says that men generally seek to avoid confrontations and blowups. How true is the conventional wisdom in your case?

Many wives build stronger relationships with their parents after marriage, while husbands tend, on the whole, to become more distant from theirs. (It's not uncommon to see the wife making an effort to maintain contact with her mother- and/or father-in-law once the husband has "detached.") And while men often put a great deal of energy and caring into the courtship period before a marriage, after the honeymoon their general tendency is to shift their top priority to work, friends, and outside interests. In extreme cases, the wife may eventually feel displaced or even abandoned. Does your relationship seem strong enough to you to withstand such stresses?

Of course, there is no hard-and-fast rule in this area. Though men and women may tend to take different approaches to certain life experiences, each individual man and woman in each individual marriage remains (thank goodness) a unique person blessed with the gifts of discretion and choice. The generalizations are helpful only in two very specific areas: setting guidelines and agreements before the marriage, so that neither partner is taken by surprise later on; and preparing for your relationship's growth over time.

Premarriage Activities

Once you've asked and answered the questions that will have most relevance to your life as a couple, what do you do next?

First, you should evaluate your partner's (and your own) answers objectively. With any luck, you'll have a better idea of who your potential mate really is, what his or her strong points are, where there are weaknesses (as there are with any human being), and how well the two of you communicate. How do you feel about what you've learned?

You probably shouldn't depend on your ability to reform a spouse. You are marrying the person you are marrying, for better or for worse, and once you are married you'll need to develop a certain amount of tolerance and a good sense of humor; in the end, you'll have to accept your partner as is. Though the approach may seem a little fatalistic, it accurately reflects the conditions of the vast majority of marriages, even the most successful ones.

Do you still feel you need more information? I've listed below a number of activities that you and your partner can try together before you make a final decision to get married. Try the ones that seem most appealing to you as a couple. Once you've completed the activity, review your experiences together. Were you comfortable together? When was there tension? How does each of you feel about your communication skills as a couple? Evaluating the activities honestly will give you a good idea of what you might expect over the course of your marriage.

Except for the last two, each of the following activities will help virtually any couple test their compatibility, regardless of whether or not an intimate sexual relationship exists.

Go on a two-week vacation, all by yourselves, to a place where you can't easily be reached. Don't visit any friends or relatives. See how well you manage.

Agree to baby-sit for friends or relatives for one full weekend or longer. (Try to arrange caring for children under the age of ten.)

Spend a day window shopping for a (hypothetical, if necessary) house or apartment full of furniture; find out where you agree and disagree on matters of taste in furnishings.

Spend two whole days in each other's company doing anything but watching television. Each of you should plan one full day's activities.

Pick a favorite relative from each partner's family to visit together.

Make a list of your traits. Each person should write what he or she considers to be the five most and five least attractive qualities of both partners. Compare notes and discuss why the lists don't agree. (They won't.)

Do a mitzvah together. (Perhaps you could work with disadvantaged children one night a week, or serve dinner at a homeless shelter.)

Spend an entire afternoon at an art or natural history museum.

Have dinner at an ethnic restaurant neither of you has tried.

Find a beautiful park, meadow, or other peaceful surrounding. Take a long walk together.

Attend and participate in *either* of the following:

a) synagogue or church services, or

b) community, political, or conservation group meetings.

For Sexually Active Partners

Vary your sexual methods. Try experimenting with new positions, settings, and times for lovemaking. If you need ideas, consult the bibliography of this book, which includes references for a number of better sex manuals. (I strongly recommend that you use a reliable contraceptive system, preferably one that incorporates a condom.)

Schedule separate professional massages, and make mental notes of the techniques used. Then, one day, give each other massages that take advantage of all you've learned. (You might do this at a time when you'd normally make love. It doesn't matter whether the massages are sexually stimulating or not.) I'm not suggesting that it will take only one session for you to become a masseur/masseuse—luckily, you don't have to be a professional to give an enjoyable massage.

On Living Together

Whether or not you decide to live together or become sexually intimate before marriage may not be a crucial factor influencing whether the marriage will succeed or not. Large-scale Canadian studies (reported by psychologist James M. White in *Psychology Today*, March 1988) suggested that cohabitants were somewhat more likely than others to stay married. Recent American studies (reported in 1989) suggest that there are more divorces after cohabitation, but as University of Pennsylvania sociologist Frank F. Furstenberg commented:

> It would be wrong to interpret these findings as saying "if people live together they are more likely to have unstable relationships." The people who are living together are different from those who aren't. They would be at more risk for having unstable relationships whether they lived together or not, given their attitudes about marriage. Are they worse off? My hunch is not.

One certain advantage of living together before marriage is that if it does not work out, you will have saved yourself a lot of trouble—however disappointed you may be.

Chapter Six:
People You Should NOT Marry

LET'S FACE THE FACTS. There are some people you would be absolutely *nuts* to marry. Some relationships will cause more pain than joy, and are unlikely to work out well for either partner.

As we all know, many marriages these days end in failure. There is no reason for you to contribute to making the statistics more depressing than they already are, by entering into a marriage that is doomed. Even if your own situation does not quite fit the category of an accident waiting to happen, you should know that there are a great many relationships that fall into a gray area. With these relationships, it may not be a bad idea to get married eventually, but both partners should think long and hard about what they want before making a commitment.

If you are involved with someone and the topic of getting married is being raised or is likely to be raised, I suggest you use the following guidelines. They may help you avoid the serious mistake of committing yourself to a destructive, exhausting, unhealthy, or just plain unsatisfying marriage.

The Don'ts

Don't marry an addict. And bear in mind that people can be "addicted" to many things other than drugs.* If your partner is an alcoholic, a drug abuser, a child molester, a womanizer, a compulsive gambler, or if he or she exhibits self-destructive/dependent behavior in any other area, do not offer to share in the dependency by getting married; neither of you will be happier for it.

You must make every effort to be honest with yourself. If your partner's behavior is compulsive (no longer voluntary), you are asking for trouble by getting married. Addicts give their addiction priority over everything else in life, including health, family, friends, and, yes, eventually even you. To make matters worse, addicts lie a lot. They also betray friends and family routinely, rarely keep promises, are big on denial, blame others (especially spouses) for their problems, and have a remarkable fondness for instant gratification over just about anything else in life. However attractive, good natured, or reasonable addicts may seem, they eventually turn out to be con artists. To marry one is to make matters worse.

If you love an addict, do not get married. A person who marries an addict becomes a co-dependent, someone who *facilitates* the negative cycle and *enhances* its harmful effects. Virtually all studies in this area indicate that your *independence* is more helpful to the addict than your co-dependence!

I am referring here mainly to someone who is in the compulsive stage, not to addicts who are recovered or recovering. With all addicts, however, one must realize that relapse is possible, even after a long time. In any case, it is usually best to decide against marrying someone in this category who has not demonstrated at least a year or so of sobriety (literal or figurative).

You can help the addict most by trying to convince him or her to seek treatment. Most (but not all) addicts will gain through par-

---

*I'm using the term "addicted" in the popular sense; it is not technically correct to refer to womanizers, gamblers, or sexual offenders as "addicts." These problems are character disorders.

ticipating in a program that uses the twelve steps of the Alcoholics Anonymous model. Ask your rabbi, clergyman, or local hot-line service for suggestions on where to go for more information on dealing with addiction.

Don't marry anyone who is violent toward you or abuses you emotionally. Husband or wife, young or old, there is no excuse for emotional or physical abuse of one's spouse. (A battered spouse is anyone who undergoes abusive or recurrent attacks, whether verbal or physical.)

It is sad but true that most battered wives started out as battered girlfriends. That's why it's so important to keep in mind that violence is the *opposite* of mature love.

If you are involved in a violent relationship, you should know that aggressive and abusive behavior is *always* a sign of despair, distress, loneliness, neurosis, and feelings of inferiority. As if that were not enough, violence can be a symptom of murderous potential; it must be taken seriously.

Why does any person stay in a violent relationship? Many women (and a surprising number of men), when asked, "Why do you stay with someone who only seems to want to hurt you?" will answer, "I love him (her)." It is more likely that the person feels unloved by anyone, has feelings of powerlessness and hopelessness, and holds a strong belief that there are simply no other options. Why anyone stays in a violent relationship is a complex question that may deserve a complex answer, but the simple answer is: No reason is good enough. If you find yourself in an abusive relationship, protect yourself—get away.

Many battered women reveal in therapy that they were abused as children, often while being lectured by a parent—along the lines of, "I'm doing this for your own good, because I love you." Further evidence suggests that the violence in relationships may run in cycles; many men who beat their wives and girlfriends were themselves abused children. But no matter what the underlying confusion may be, if you work on an abusive partner's recovery, do so from a safe distance, preferably under the supervision of a professional.

If you're ever attacked physically by the person who claims to love you, draw the line then and there. My advice is to be prepared to forgive, but with a warning. Tell your partner flatly that if the violence ever makes a return appearance, you are gone; that's it. Then stick to your word. You might be willing to listen to the promises to atone—once. After that, it is time to move on, to a relative or conceivably to one of the available shelters for battered spouses, and perhaps to therapy (often the remedy for the violent spouse, as well). Though it may be difficult and frightening to take the first step, the sad fact is that remaining in a violent relationship is a life-threatening proposition.

Don't "marry" someone who's already married. In other words, don't count on a married person divorcing his or her spouse and then marrying you.

I am not going to tell you that it is impossible to form a lifelong relationship with someone who's already married. But I can tell you that the odds aren't very encouraging. In the vast majority of cases, the "secondary" relationship doesn't work out. Most of the men and women who have affairs with married people . . . have affairs with married people. And that's it. The encounters are just interludes, flings—not serious relationships.

Most people do not give up their marriages over affairs. (Of course, it's another matter if your lover is already separated and waiting for a divorce to be finalized.) But the temptation for many still exists to try to find fulfillment in these relationships; too often, the results are tragic.

I'm often asked if there is any reliable way to tell if the married lover (usually a man) is "really serious." In my view, the best way to estimate the odds of such a relationship working out is to be brutally honest and gauge the time preference of the married partner. If he or she is in the process of leaving a dying relationship, and still tends to spend weekends away from you, leaving time only for brief encounters, that's not an encouraging signal.

People who play games make mistakes. They tell lies; they make promises they cannot keep; they have lots of secrets; they make you wait on street corners. People who aren't serious are preoccupied with themselves; they forget important occasions in your life; they can't seem to remember things that should be important to both of you.

Other Risk Groups

Apart from the broader guidelines I've set out above, you'll want to consider whether you or your potential spouse falls into certain high-risk categories, groups that are, generally speaking, more likely to end up divorcing than the rest of the population. Many marriages end unhappily not because the spouses are inherently bad but simply because they neglect, before committing to marriage, to examine carefully the many factors that influence relationships over time.

Do Not Marry . . .

. . . if you are both still young. Marriages between two partners who are under twenty-one are more likely than not to end in divorce or separation.

. . . if you feel you have a bad relationship with either of your parents and your prospective spouse seems to you to be someone just like that parent.

. . . if the partners consistently seem to have difficulty accepting each other's ideas, fight most of the time, or simply do not appear to understand each other.

. . . if conversations frequently contain any of the following phrases: "Do you really love me?" "Are you sure it's me you love?" "I wish you were more like . . ." "You have to give up *those* friends. We can only have mutual friends now." "I can't stand it when you spend time alone reading (pursuing a hobby) (meditating) (whatever). You should spend every minute you can with me."

. . . if your decision to get married has been heavily influenced by either partner's parents. Many people, seduced by the acceptance, flattery, wealth or even cooking of a potential in-law, find themselves at the altar promising to spend their lives with someone for whom they do not have any genuine feelings.

. . . if your partner has traits you abhor (such as a violent temper or poor grooming habits), yet you find yourself unable to raise the issue for fear of offending.

. . . if you find yourself being too anxious to please a partner who gives little in return, or you feel he or she makes consistently selfish demands and rarely considers your welfare.

. . . if, after extensive discussion, you're still unable to agree on where you're going to live or under what circumstances (i.e., career changes or new income opportunities elsewhere) you would move in the future.

. . . if your values regarding material goods are radically different. Couples often have major conflicts when they realize, after getting married, that one spouse prefers a modest standard of living while the other insists on lavish surroundings and a steady ascent up the ladder of success.

. . . if either of you is desperate to marry as soon as possible. If only for your own sake, don't marry anyone out of panic or pressure from another person. No matter who is applying the pressure, and no matter what the reason (pregnancy, the need to leave home, a ticking biological clock, the desire to fit in with all your married friends, loneliness, fear of independence, or any of the other possibilities), it is always best to delay a decision to get married if anything has convinced you that you must walk down the altar immediately. (In addition, you should be alert if your partner becomes so preoccupied with wedding plans that you feel neglected—as though it's not happening to you.)

For further suggestions on the difficult job of establishing whether or not your relationship can support a lifetime commitment, consult the bibliography at the end of this book. It will supply you with the titles of some excellent books in the field. Don't be put off if a book addresses itself to women if you're a man, or vice versa; I particularly recommend those books that allow the reader to get a glimpse of how the opposite sex views the problems and issues surrounding love, commitment, and relationships.

On the Fence

While there are many people you should not marry, there is a special category of people about whom it is particularly hard to make a judgment one way or the other: I call these people fence-sitters.

These are the on-again/off-again people who postpone engagements or constantly hedge about the subject of getting married; they're afraid of making a commitment. Many reasons may underlie this fear.

A lot of people look for perfection in a mate—and nobody's perfect. Some fence-sitters are afraid of making a mistake in choosing a mate, always convinced that somebody better is out there waiting to be discovered. Others are reluctant to lose their independence or say goodbye to the freedom and good times they have known or imagined. Still others are fearful of responsibility and anticipate the worst in everything, asking themselves how they will cope with all the crises that loom in the future: "What if I lose my job? What if we can't pay the mortgage? What if our child is born retarded?"

Then there are people who always seem to be preoccupied with what others might think and use other people's opinions as an excuse to delay a decision. Their own judgments or evaluations never carry as much weight as those of the outside world: "He is not handsome enough for my crowd." "My parents aren't doing cartwheels over her, that's for sure." "Marrying him might make me happy, but as far as prestige goes, it wouldn't be much of a catch compared to the guy my sister ended up with." Marriage is difficult enough when you only have to satisfy each other.

All of this puts the fence-sitter's partner on a precarious perch. When are the indecisive person's objections legitimate, and when are they simply shields against a choice? Does the inability to come to a decision indicate that there's a likelihood of future problems in the marriage? What do you do if you're really in love with a fence sitter, one you feel strongly about marrying?

Indecision Is a Decision to Fail

The only way out of ambivalence is to make a decision. Once you have made every effort to talk through all the issues and problems surrounding your relationship, set a deadline for an answer one way or the other. While this may well lead to an emotionally charged situation, remember that you won't be asking for anything unreasonable—just an answer to a big question, so that you can get on with your life.

So, keep in mind that a "no" answer is not necessarily a reason for you to terminate either the friendship or the love relationship. Though you may need to take some time on your own, or have genuine feelings of disappointment to deal with, there is no reason to burn bridges. Most of us can use all the friends we can get. On the other hand, ending the relationship might be the best thing that could happen to both of you. Make the decision in terms of what is best for you.

Other Judgment Calls

Like the fence-sitter, there are a number of other categories of people who deserve close scrutiny before you decide to spend your life with them. You should consider marrying, but be very careful about the following people.

A divorced person. Half of all previously divorced people will divorce again. When it comes to failed marriages, there is a definite tendency to make the same mistake more than once. Unfortunately, many divorced people do not examine why their previous marriages did not work.

If you are considering marrying a person who has been divorced, try to discuss the problems of the previous marriage in depth. Ask your partner why he or she feels that this time around will be different—and see what elements of the relationship will be the same.

If the partner's response is something along the lines of "I don't want to talk about it," watch out. You're being shown a very clear danger signal, and you should proceed with the utmost caution.

Before marrying a divorced person, make sure that all agreements with the ex-spouse are in writing and that you have reviewed these agreements carefully. You wouldn't believe the disasters you can find yourself walking into when there are significant unresolved conflicts between a divorced couple, especially conflicts regarding children.

Though they are certainly not among the best ways to begin a marriage, fights between your partner and his or her former spouse may well come with the territory, and you should be aware of any serious disagreements before you decide to get married. Whatever else you do, discuss the issue openly and settle on a strategy that will help you cope. Stay above the fray. If you do not remain polite, non-threatening, and calm, your presence will make matters worse. Stay away from trials and court proceedings if at all possible. (Obviously, marrying a divorced person with children presents many challenges. I'll deal with the thorny issue of making a healthy adjustment to an adopted family in more detail later on in this book.)

A widow or widower. If the previous marriage was relatively good, then your chances for success in marrying a widow or widower are better than if you were marrying a divorced person. However, you should be prepared for the possibility that your spouse will eventually make some unfavorable comparisons between you and his or her previous mate. A deceased spouse may be idealized by the survivor. There may even be interludes of fantasy and denial.

Your goal will be to remind your mate gently that everyone is unique, and that it is unrealistic and unfair for him or her to expect to reenter the previous marriage. This relationship should represent a new experience, a new opportunity, a chance to begin again. If you feel that regular, unflattering comparisons with someone you'll never be able to surpass are going to be a permanent component of the marriage, think seriously about how happy you will be in such a situation.

Someone significantly older or younger than you. There isn't necessarily any serious problem in marrying when the age difference is more than ten years, but it's a good idea for both of you to be aware of the long-range barriers that may present themselves (i.e., "When he is fifty, I will be thirty-five"). It is also important to look for hidden agendas and unspoken motivations. Are there factors at work that neither person has admitted (for instance, money or status)? Does the relationship encourage good communication? If there are mothering or fathering tendencies, how do you feel about this?

Someone who has a serious handicap. Examine your motivations here, as well. In a mature relationship, as long as considerations of financial gain, or pity, for instance, don't enter into the picture, and as long as all the sensitive issues relating to topics like sexuality and long-term care have been addressed openly, there is as good a chance for success as there is with any other match.

Someone who is bisexual or homosexual. Is a mature marriage possible with someone who is bisexual or homosexual? Many homosexuals, and perhaps a majority of bisexuals, marry. If the thousands of enthusiastic letters received by Ann Landers upon addressing the issue in a recent column are any indication, many such marriages are successful. The key here, as you might imagine, is honesty. Each partner must disclose the relevant facts about his or her sexuality, and there must be clear agreement regarding what constitutes acceptable behavior. It is surprising to many people, but there are some very good marriages that don't feature superlative sex as their central element.

Marriages to homosexuals usually fail when honesty is lacking, and often in the context of the "secret" being discovered in explosive circumstances—in much the same way that a heterosexual marriage may self-destruct if one partner engages in a secret, long-term affair and is caught.

No one should consider marriage to a homosexual or a bisexual, or to any other risk group member, without insisting that the partner be tested for the HIV antibody (which reveals the presence of the virus that is responsible for AIDS).

Someone with a different religious background. Interfaith marriages are more common now than they used to be. Even if both partners are nonaffiliated and nonpracticing, however, such couples stand a greater chance of divorcing than couples who are of the same religion.

When people from different religious backgrounds first announce that they intend to marry, tensions are often high; frequently, parents object. In the end, the decision to marry is usually accepted by all parties. It's later on that most of the most significant problems emerge. What religion will the children practice? How should the couple deal with relatives and friends still very committed to their own religion? Which holidays will be celebrated, and with what foods? Often, the compromises attempted comfort no one. (Many Jews, for example, frown on couples who celebrate both Christmas and Hanukkah.)

It is easier to marry someone with whom you're compatible who also shares your background. Nevertheless, marrying a person you love is infinitely preferable to marrying someone you don't, religion or no religion. I encourage interfaith couples to discuss all the relevant issues fully and openly, to consider seriously the option of formal conversion (probably to the minority religion), and to be prepared for ongoing examination of the challenges inherent to such marriages. The picture for interfaith couples need not be a discouraging one: at the very least, interfaith marriage is an occasion for the religious education of the couple in both religious traditions.

Chapter Seven:
Letting Go

IF THE PAIN of being with the person you love far outweighs the joy you share . . .

If your love is more of a burden than a pleasure . . .

If you feel desperate or lonely when you are with your partner, but closer to him or her, somehow, when you're apart . . .

If you're terrified at the thought of never finding anyone else . . .

If your partner bullies you and brings you to a point of despair . . .

Then it's time to let go of your relationship.

Easier Said Than Done

Extricating oneself from a destructive and/or painful relationship is one of the most difficult tasks we face in life. And it's a lot easier to talk about than it is to do. But when it must be done, there is nothing to be gained by avoiding the issue.

In this chapter we will take a look at some of the problems facing people in troubled love relationships and examine some of the options available that will allow both of you to uncouple and move on.

A victimized or unsatisfied partner may have been experiencing frustration, anger, and pain for years—without ever developing the tools necessary to let go. What stands in the way? There are many possible answers, and many defenses offered in hopes of maintaining the status quo.

"I love him (her)." (Probably. But there is also a very good chance that an overriding characteristic of the relationship is the inability to support mutual, mature love and affection.)

"My partner has threatened to commit suicide." (Though you can certainly have sympathy for someone undergoing an emotional crisis, this is still no reason to stay in a bad relationship. If you are really worried, be sure that your partner's family and/or friends know about your feelings. Delay announcing your intent to leave—at least until you have made sure that he or she is in a safe place.)

"It will break his (her) heart." (People get over pain and suffering a lot faster when you deal with them honestly, rather than continuing to foster an environment that doesn't represent reality. You have genuine needs. Express them. Staying in a bad relationship will do neither of you any good in the long run.)

"At least this way, I will be financially secure." (Are you sure about that? Are you sure you are not being drained for all you are worth? Are you sure your only option is to continue along the same path, even though it is making you miserable? Have you honestly examined other resources, such as employment and training programs or support groups?)

"I'm frightened; if I leave, I may be alone for the rest of my life." (If you make the effort to be honest with yourself, you will probably recognize that you are quite lonely right now. And you are likely to get lonelier: the longer you live with someone you do not like—or worse, someone you hate—the lonelier you will be.)

How do you let go of a destructive relationship and get on with your life?

First, take the time to think things through. Review what you feel is the least satisfying or the most threatening aspect of the relationship. Then determine the two or three aspects of your life with your partner that are the most painful or difficult for you to tolerate. (If there are more than three, select the three most important.) Make a list. Get very specific.

In private, take the time to go over the items in detail. Memorize them, so that it will not be possible for you to forget what you want to talk about.

Then, when you feel confident that you've isolated exactly what makes the relationship difficult for you, take time to sit down with your mate and talk it out. In beginning the process, be attentive to the setting you choose, to timing, and to your partner's frame of mind. If you've decided to leave because your partner drinks too much and is abusive when intoxicated, it is not a good idea to announce your departure when he or she has come home at two in the morning dead drunk.

Say clearly that you now find it too difficult and too stressful to continue the relationship unless there is rapid and noticeable improvement in certain areas. Then outline the problems you identified earlier.

Try to do this without attacking or assuming a confrontational attitude. It will not help your position to make cruel remarks about your partner's personality or potential. Just tell the truth as you see it.

It will be easier for you if you can anticipate reactions and be ready to answer them. I have listed a number of possible reactions and responses below.

"Why are you doing this to me?" I am doing this for myself.

"I can't live without you." I have to be able to live with myself. I can't go on with broken promises, and I can't keep trying to

make a relationship work when it is so painful and unproductive.

"I love you and you hate me." Of course I love you; but love isn't enough to keep a relationship going. Being able to trust you counts, too. Being able to know you'll be there for me, that you care enough to try to change (problem), that you want to help me and not just have me help you . . . all of that counts. Those things matter just as much as love in a relationship, and ours doesn't work because those things aren't there. I have to do this; we aren't good for each other right now.

If you are not certain that the relationship should be terminated, you can take a middle course—outline the problems, then set a deadline for genuine change (say, one month). If, after that period of time, there has been no improvement, you'll be perfectly justified in telling your partner that your own sanity and dignity demand that you let go. Another option is to force counseling, suggesting that this course of action represents your last compromise.

The Aftermath

After you've broken up, don't rush out to find another romance. Take some time to bounce back emotionally. Your life has undergone a significant change. Take as long as necessary to put all the pieces back and get a good idea of who the new, independent you really is.

Reflect on the experience. What can you learn from it? Consider keeping a notebook of your observations during this crucial period.

Review the ideas in chapters one and two and make new efforts to improve yourself, learn new things, and do mitzvahs. In addition, you might put new effort into developing any friendships with those you have been neglecting. Again, try to concentrate on same-sex friends. Do not pressure yourself to become romantically involved.

You will go through periods of unhappiness, loneliness, and pain. This is natural and should not be misinterpreted as a sign that you belong back in the unhealthy relationship. If, after a while, your situation does not improve, try to get counseling or join a support group.

Take the blame where appropriate; if you convince yourself you were not responsible for anything, then you have no control over the same patterns emerging the next time around. Draw the line of reason and reality and avoid blame for what you did not do. No one is ever totally at fault in any failed relationship; every breakup is a complex failure, some of which can be traced to one person or the other, and some of which cannot.

Albert Ellis, in his excellent book, *How to Stubbornly Refuse to Make Yourself Miserable About Anything—Yes, Anything!* offers helpful suggestions in this area:

> If you are disappointed and regretful about being rejected by a love partner, you will try to discover why you were abandoned, to win back that person's love, or to attempt to mate with a more suitable partner. But if you are angry at your rejector, you will antagonize him or her and remain an enemy instead of a friend.

This is a learning time. You are adding to your knowledge of the way things work in human relationships, even during your most difficult moments. Among the things you'll have the chance to learn now is the stark fact that many of the cliches that surround love, the phrases that may ring bitterly in your ears in your relationship's aftermath, are just that—cliches. Opposites do not necessarily attract. Love is not necessarily forever. Love cannot conquer all. And most important of all: Love is not blind.

Proceed from the assumption that you are a good person, with or without this relationship. In time, wounds will heal and scars will fade.

Interlude:
Taking Stock

NOW IT IS TIME to take a look at yourself.

If you've tried some of the ideas I outlined earlier in the book, and you feel better about yourself and your relationships with others—great! If, however, you feel that you're struggling, or that noticeable results have been slow in coming, we'll take a look at some of the possible reasons why (and suggest some alternatives) in this chapter.

What is Standing in the Way?

There are a number of contributing reasons for people having difficulty doing well in their relationships with others.

They have difficulty seeing and focusing on the needs of others. (This is where mitzvahs can help!)

They appear boring. (Because they have not invested the time to acquire passionate interests.)

They talk too much. (Usually about themselves and the injustices visited upon them by the cruel world at large.)

They don't say much to anybody. (They believe they don't have anything interesting to contribute to the conversation . . . a self-fulfilling prophecy.)

They are overly critical of others or blame innocent people for problems and mistakes. (A universally unattractive quality.)

They do not keep confidences. (It's hard to get close to someone who has a history of repeating your most intimate secrets to anyone who will listen.)

They bombard themselves with negative messages. (Like, "All the good people are married.")

They are angry because other people have hurt them. (Forgiveness? This crowd wants revenge, and they do not want to discuss anything else, thank you.)

They are paralyzed by the prospect of risk. (Meanwhile, they risk a lifetime of loneliness and bitterness by not reaching out to and making contact with someone.)

They feel that they are so superior that nobody can measure up to them. (In actuality, they are too selfish to form a mutually satisfying relationship.)

The Major Reason

There is one underlying problem common to virtually every one of the roadblocks I have just described: low self-esteem. Remember Eleanor Roosevelt's observation that "No one can make you feel inferior without your consent"? Now it is time to address the enduring question of precisely why so many people habitually buy into feelings of inferiority.

Everybody has *tzuris* (Yiddish for "troubles"), but people who feel inferior seem to have more than their share. Perhaps the heart of the problem lies in the way such people look at themselves.

How you feel about who you are is a tremendously important factor in projecting long-term happiness. What messages do you send out about yourself? What arbitrary half-truths do you accept about yourself? Do you want to believe them? To what degree are they inaccurate?

There are, in my view, seven "cardinal sins" that will eventually enable you to convince yourself that you are unattractive, uninteresting, laden with serious character defects, and unable to sustain a mature relationship. And by the time you are finished convincing yourself that they describe you accurately, you will probably be right.

One: Constantly comparing yourself to others. Yes. There will always be individuals who appear to be more handsome, richer, luckier, or better educated than you are. Unfortunately, none of them has the privilege of being you. That's their tough luck. There will always be individuals who appear to be uglier, poorer, less fortunate and more ignorant than you are. Unfortunately, that fact makes you neither brighter nor better.

Each of us is unique. Each of us is special. Each person has a vital mission in life, which no one else is so perfectly equipped to accomplish. One of the most revered Jewish sages, Reb Zusya, is reported to have said on his deathbed, "God will not ask me why I was not like Moses. He will ask me why I wasn't myself."

No matter how beautiful or successful someone else appears to be, *only you have your own place and your own mission.* We are all unique individuals, destined to serve God (or, if you prefer, humanity or life) in a special way. And if you think that fulfilling your mission is a self-centered activity, there are thousands of years of scholarship, philosophy, and theology that suggest a different conclusion. Many Hassidic Jews, for example, believe, that the reason the Messiah has not arrived is that somewhere, one or more people are not trying hard enough to fulfill the universal purpose of serving the Almighty.

Two: Believing that you won't amount to much unless you get married. Unless someone falls in love with you. Unless someone needs you. Unless you make lots of money. Unless you please your parents.

The fact is, these preconditions are usually impossible to fulfill. As long as you define yourself in terms of other people, external achievements, or goals to reach, there is really no *you* to love.

You have to be *someone* to attract anyone. You must accept yourself before you can please those you care to please. If you do not amount to anything before someone wants you, you will not amount to much afterward.

Three: Attempting to please everyone. Thinking that you can satisfy all the people with whom you come into contact over the course of your life is dangerous. I believe that the apparent paradox of selfishness was addressed and resolved in the first century B.C., when Rabbi Hillel asked: "If I am not for myself, who will be for me? If I am only for myself, what am I?" (Perkai Avot, Sayings of the Fathers [1:14])

You must first please yourself. After that, you can work on making the people you care about happy. Beyond that, you're unlikely to do much more than ensure dissatisfaction with yourself, because there's always going to be someone who'll grumble that you're not doing enough. Let them grumble and don't take yourself to task for it. People who try to please everyone end up pleasing no one.

Four: Being a perfectionist with unrealistic goals. Many people think of themselves as failures because they're unable to achieve wildly ambitious objectives. If this describes you, you can improve your performance in any area you choose by starting out with a more modest, attainable goal.

Remember, you can always raise tomorrow's goal, after you have achieved today's. People do not graduate from college and immediately become well known in their field. There are steps that have to be taken in between those points. Take the same attitude in your relationships. Do not expect your partner to fulfill every dream you have ever had from day one. Start small. Work your way up—together.

Five: Expecting that the meaning of life will become clear in a good relationship. Life is not a meaning. Life is an opportunity for meaningful experiences. You can only take part in meaningful experiences. You will only have the perspective to perceive the ultimate meaning of your life at the end of it. Don't rush it.

Do not expect instant answers to the broad questions or profound lessons from thirty-second commercials. Some of the most profound things about relationships are intimately related to our mundane, everyday existence. Life is made up of meaningful experiences, not definitive answers. Those experiences are often of short duration, but they can occur again and again . . . and in that cycle one can find pleasure and fulfillment.

Six: Cultivating boredom as a way of life. Some people, it seems, find a great deal of comfort in being bored. How else can you explain their relentless attachment to the very things that bore them?

If you're bored, you're boring to be with. And you're not only boring for others to be with, you'll be boring for *you* to be with! If continued attempts to find a passionate, challenging interest lead you nowhere, then, by all means, *fake it* for a while. *Pretend* you're enthralled with what's taking place, and see what happens. Moaning about how you have nothing to do or how uninteresting an activity is will always make you less attractive and lower your self-image.

Seven: Believing that forces outside of yourself control your life. It's interesting to note that people who feel this way tend not to take very good care of themselves.

Such attitudes do not do much for the way others look at you, and they certainly don't do much for a healthy self-image. Even though there are uncertainties and experiences over which you have no control in life, ultimately, *you* are responsible for your existence. It has to be you. If it is not you—if job, family, politics, weather, or anything else has the final word about who you are, what you do, and how you can feel about things—then you've effectively abdicated your role in your own life.

The Paradox

Worried about your appearance? Don't start from the outside. Start with the inside.

You can apply all the face cream, deodorant, hair conditioner, and makeup you want; you must still care about yourself before you can expect mature love in return. This is something of a paradox. Many people are surprised when they learn that the best way to attract someone else is to pay healthy, continuous, non-narcissistic attention to themselves. But it is true. If you develop a positive self-image, other people will be attracted to you. People who feel good about themselves do not exploit others and are not available for exploitation. People who feel good about themselves, far from exhausting or trying the patience of their acquaintances, exhibit a veritable feast of exciting, appealing characteristics that other human beings tend to find irresistible.

Don't misunderstand me; there are some people who feel good about themselves but are basically mean, selfish, and hostile. Their "feeling good about themselves" is often a cover for basic character defects. These people aren't enjoyable to be with and are easily recognized as phonies. (A California legislative task force developed a definition of self-esteem that I like: "Appreciating my own worth and importance, and having the character to be accountable for myself and to act responsibly towards others.")

So even if you do not feel good about yourself, the very best way to move yourself in a positive direction is to do mitzvahs—to be helpful to others, especially those who are less fortunate than yourself.

People Who Are Self-accepting . . .

. . . laugh.

. . . listen.

. . . do not exploit others for their own gratification.

. . . have energy.

. . . are more creative than people who hold themselves in low esteem.

. . . are tolerant of the changing moods of others.

. . . learn to live with what they cannot change.

. . . exude enthusiasm.

. . . project confidence.

. . . exult in the successes of their friends without feeling competitive or threatened.

. . . are sensitive to the needs of others.

. . . take appropriate risks.

. . . risk failure in order to find out what they have the right stuff for.

. . . often have an intriguing sense of depth or mystery about them.

. . . do not pretend to have all the answers.

. . . are realistically optimistic.

. . . do not ridicule the helpless or humiliate the weak.

. . . tend to make people they spend time with feel good about themselves.

. . . enjoy helping others and working to develop a sense of community.

. . . have a sense of purpose and develop the sense of a special mission in life.

. . . are able to turn their mistakes into lessons and begin anew.

Don't kid yourself; even people who exhibit most, if not all, of the above characteristics suffer periods of despair, disappointment, and depression. Bad things do happen to good people, even those with a healthy sense of self-worth. But such people rebound.

It is all very well to talk about the importance of self-esteem, but developing and maintaining high self-esteem takes effort for everyone, and it is a very difficult, uphill struggle for many people (including many extremely accomplished people). Change does not take place overnight. But by focusing on attainable goals, and by rededicating our strength to realizing them, we strengthen the way we see ourselves.

It may look as if it would take a miracle for you to fundamentally change the way you look at yourself. OK. Start creating that miracle by taking a long look at you. Recognize that you are a unique human being—not perfect, unique. Realize that no one else on this earth has exactly what you have to offer. Reinforce that positive fact; believe that you are good enough, all in all, to stand on your own merits. Compare yourself to yourself; judge your actions against your own capabilities and resources. Learn to see yourself in your own light and you will be fine. Eventually, the destructive and debilitating urge to compare yourself with others will become less meaningful. Remember that the presumed advantages of others are of no significance to you. They cannot triumph over your tragedies. They cannot grow to be the mature, productive you only you can become.

Keep in mind the old Zen expression: "When the mind is ready, a teacher appears."

Are you ready?

Chapter Eight
Sex—How Important Is It?

IN CONTEMPORARY AMERICAN society, sex has been ruthlessly commercialized, consistently overstated in relation to its actual role in our lives, and shamelessly sensationalized at every opportunity.

With so many of us awash in this sea of adolescent titillation, is it any wonder we are often confused about our sexuality?

We are bombarded daily with silly sexual messages and stereotypes. The sources are legion: billboard after billboard, commercial after commercial, rock video after rock video, book after book, and film after film, we are told, directly or indirectly, that sex constitutes the most significant aspect of modern life.

The irony is that the vast majority of the messages we receive are *antisexual* in nature. Why? Because most of the images the media presents have nothing to do with ordinary or healthy sexual experiences.

Think about it. It is extremely rare for a television drama to treat the topic of love (with or without sexual expression) in a mature or even moderately enlightened way. Much more common are portrayals of people as lustful brutes or childish buffoons in their relationships, which accent, wherever possible, the exploitative aspects of sexuality. Rape, adultery, sadomasochism, and violence get a far greater percentage of the attention than caring and compassionate interactions.

Equally troubling is the advertising industry's seemingly unquenchable desire to establish and reinforce impossible standards of physical allure and sexual persuasiveness. To take the advertisers at face value is to believe that every woman must be stunningly (and identically) beautiful, that every man will seduce an attractive woman given the slightest chance, and that only the purchase of the toothpaste, perfume, clothing, or cosmetic in question will allow one to lead a satisfying sex life.

Perhaps it is because of such messages that so many people use sex as a bargaining tool, or (just as troubling) as a way to avoid intimacy, rather than express it. Many people in our society reject sex as a pleasurable sharing experience, opting instead to use it as proof of manhood or femininity, or as a back door to satisfy deep-seated desires related to being wanted or validated as a person. That such approaches to sexuality are still common is disturbing, and, considering the recent upswings in the rate and severity of sexually transmitted diseases, downright alarming.

In the broad sense, all of us are sexual in many, many aspects of life, and sexuality *is* of great importance to us as men and women—but it needs to be viewed as one of the many dimensions of our existence. As I've already indicated, I believe that of the ten most important aspects of a relationship, sex ranks ninth. (Most couples in a happy, mature relationship will tell you that the strongest turn-on is intimacy, and that love and caring can, in their own ways, be more rewarding and exciting than the simple act of intercourse.)

There are, in my opinion, four key ideas that will help us put sex into its proper perspective; in this chapter, we'll look at each in detail.

Four Guidelines

One: Sexual intercourse is neither a test nor a proof of love. I've mentioned this before, but the point is so routinely ignored that it bears repeating. Caring about each other, sharing unselfishly, developing respect for your partner—these are the things that will help you build a strong relationship, one that will stand the test of time. Simply going to bed together will, on its own, prove nothing.

It's quite common today for couples to undergo serious crises that have at their root a confusion of sex and love.

Perhaps the most familiar example of this is the teenaged couple entering the first stages of sexual experimentation. The young woman is told by her partner that if she really loved him, she'd have sex with him. If the young man's demands don't confuse sex with love, nothing does.

There are other such scenarios. Consider the case of a young, happily married couple who have just celebrated their first anniversary. After a full year of trying, they are still unable to achieve simultaneous orgasms (an unrealistic goal for most couples). They consider this a slowly worsening catastrophe. Do they really love each other after all? Did they make some terrible mistake in getting married?

Or how about the couple, happily married for fifteen years, who have the misfortune to read about the newest trendy "disease" to make an appearance in the newsweeklies—lack of sexual desire? "How often," they now ask themselves, "*do* we make love, anyway?" Here they thought they were a contented couple! They were foolish enough to believe that the steady growth of intimacy, understanding, and caring they'd experienced was a good sign. Now they're asked to believe that those things only masked some terrible disorder that is now keeping them from having the right amount of sex together! (Of course, there is no right amount of lovemaking, and the couple described has no need to consult a sex therapist or marriage counselor.)

Sex and love, then, must not be confused. It's a good idea to remember that there are people who have perfectly good, or even ecstatic, sexual relationships with partners they loathe. There are also couples who are very deeply in love, but whose sex lives aren't particularly satisfying for them because of problems such as impotence, inability to reach orgasm, or premature ejaculation. And yes, there are even people (wonder of wonders!) who have completely mature, exciting relationships with no such physical problems, in which sexual intercourse occurs rarely and is of minimal consequence.

Of course, millions of well-adjusted couples enjoy buoyant, frequent sexual intercourse as part of a well-rounded, caring, and intimate relationship. But that does not mean that their love for their partners is any guarantee of ongoing sexual frequency or satisfaction.

Two: There's absolutely nothing wrong with waiting until you're married to have sex. Nevertheless, some important facts should be taken into account. First, if you do decide to wait, you should know that you are most definitely in the minority. It's been estimated that less than one-tenth of all newlyweds are both virgins on their wedding night. The National Center for Health Statistics reported in 1985 that four out of five women had sex before marriage. And my own research suggests that something in the neighborhood of ninety percent of all men are sexually active before they're married.

In addition, if you decide to postpone sex until marriage, you must be prepared for the possibility that the earth will not move nor the skies part on that first night. If you expect to have simultaneous orgasms the first time, you're likely to come away from the experience feeling an emotion something akin to, "For *this* I waited?"

Sexual technique is something people learn, not something they're born with, and first experiences tend to be grim for both sexes. The standard reactions for most men after first coitus is that the experience was embarrassing; for most women, that it was painful.

Finally, let me caution you against the double standard in this area. It is foolish and unfair to reduce a potential partner to a category by placing undue emphasis on whether or not he or she is a virgin.

After one of my lectures, a young man approached me; after some discussion about what makes for a satisfying relationship, our conversation turned to his marital plans. I asked him what kind of person would make him happy, and he immediately ruled out any woman with any prior sexual experience whatsoever. "I'm a man," he said, "so naturally I fool around. But, when I get married I'm going to settle down with a virgin."

"I hope," I told him, "that you will marry a person, and not a hymen."

Three: Partners can only learn the most important things about sex from each other, and that means good communication is essential. Not too long ago, a woman who had been married for ten years complained to me that she'd never had an orgasm because her husband had no idea how to stimulate her. "Why don't you show him how?" I asked. "Oh, I couldn't," she replied. "I don't want to hurt his feelings."

I'm all for tact and politeness, but basic human needs are basic human needs, and if they are consistently ignored, something is wrong somewhere. Specifically, something is probably wrong with this couple's communication skills.

Are you hesitant about discussing what does or does not satisfy you sexually? Do you (or would you) rebuff attempts to communicate about sex? Do you think that sex takes care of itself without either partner having to provide feedback? If so, you may be on the road to a crisis—one you can easily avoid.

Once you can talk openly about your reactions to sex, you and your partner will have opened up a new world of intimacy and togetherness. Doing so is worth the initial feelings of awkwardness and risk, which usually pass in time.

Four: The best way to test any relationship's potential is to postpone having sex. It's true. What do you do in the meantime? Plenty!

Sexual intercourse, as you may have gathered by now, is not the only way in which people express their sexuality. The other options are virtually limitless. Hugging, kissing, foot or body massages, long walks holding hands (yes, I said holding hands)— all are healthy ways to express physical attraction.

Ann Landers, in a recent column, reported on thousands upon thousands of letters she had received from women who claimed that they would gladly give up sex if they could be sure of receiving from their partners, in exchange, satisfying levels of nonsexual physical affection: caresses, kisses, and hugs. Of course, most women would prefer both sex and intimacy. But apparently the letter-writers were getting quite enough sex and not enough of what they wanted—the caring and tenderness which, too often, does not accompany coitus.

It's also interesting to note that a standard treatment for people who have sexual problems is not to have sex for a month or longer. During that time the couple builds communication skills; they talk about what is or is not physically satisfying about their lovemaking; they try out alternative sexual expressions like those outlined above. Most important, the partners give themselves the chance to discover (or rediscover) the beauty and wonder of each other's personalities.

Sex: The Lifelong Learning Experience

I would like to offer a few more important points on the larger issue of human sexuality itself. I should point out, though, that the topic as a whole is vast and ever-changing. Sex is a lifelong learning experience, one that cannot be fully and completely addressed in any book, much less within a few pages. (For more in-depth approaches, consult the bibliography.) What follows, then, are brief (and, I hope, helpful) observations on some of the more important questions and problems relating to sexuality today.

Fantasies

First, let's talk about fantasies. Many people are curious about their sexual fantasies, but they fail to work up the necessary courage or self-acceptance to ask the question that is on their minds: Am I thinking normal thoughts?

The answer is yes. Behavior, of course, can be right or wrong, but thought in itself cannot. We all have oddball thoughts, bizarre dreams, and outlandish fantasies, along with frivolous wishes and forbidden sexual desires. They often come from the unconscious mind, leaving us with little or no control over the way they merge into our consciousness. That's OK.

If you allow yourself to feel guilty about a particular turn-on, it will probably repeat itself for as long as you continue to tell yourself that the thought was wrong. Why? Because guilt is powerful; guilt energizes the repetition of unaccepted thoughts, which can lead to unacceptable behavior.

Once you realize that all fantasies, no matter how off-the-wall, are a normal part of human existence, they will pass harmlessly on and give you no further trouble.

In *my* fantasy life, I'm a "trisexual," one who has tried everything. But like most people, I draw a clear line between the real world (in which my actions must be responsible ones) and the world of dreams and desires.

Of course, when normal thoughts become obsessions, they can influence you negatively or upset the pattern of your life. Nevertheless, it is the *action* that needs to be controlled, not the fantasy.

Teen Sex

In my view, it is perfectly proper to discourage teenagers from having sexual intercourse.

Why am I against teen sex? As a rule, teenagers are too young, too vulnerable, and far too likely to end up the victims of abuse or exploitation. Furthermore, when teenagers do have sex, they tend not to use contraceptives.

Teenagers represent the group most likely to be unable to handle the consequences of a sexual relationship. If you feel the same way, and want to make early efforts to avoid future crises, you may want to read my book, *Raising a Child Conservatively in a Sexually Permissive World* (revised and updated edition, Fireside, 1989), where the topic is treated in detail.

Penis Size: It Means Less Than You Think

Freud may have gotten it wrong when he wrote about women having penis envy. In contemporary society it seems that only men have it.

Penis size is, in the overwhelming majority of cases, unrelated to sexual gratification, no matter what you hear and no matter how sensitive some men are about the issue. Size is not what counts. The desire to satisfy each other is what counts. Furthermore, one cannot tell the size of the penis by observing its nonerect state. Some appear small, yet erect to six inches; others appear large, yet erect to five-and-a-half inches. One size, as it were, fits all.

Along the same lines, it's worth noting that a mature vagina can't be "too small." After all, a *baby* comes out through the vagina! While tension or nervousness may be the cause of enough tightness or rigidity to make sex difficult, no vagina is too small for a penis.

Sexual Gamesmanship

While many people are making a commitment to genuine compassion and caring in their relationships, there is still a lot of gameplaying when it comes to sex. How do you respond to such sexual manipulation?

In my book, *Seduction Lines Heard 'Round the World—And Answers You Can Give* (Prometheus, 1987), I collected hundreds of lines that men and women use to seduce one another (men still lead the field), and I supplied some comebacks for use in responding to these lines.

Here are some examples.

C'mon, everybody's doing it.
Good. Then you won't have any trouble finding someone else to do it with.

Where have you been all my life?
Hiding from you.

I can't use a condom. I get no feeling that way.
That's strange, all the other guys I know get plenty of feeling with a condom.

If I put on a condom, I won't get the right sensation out of our lovemaking.
If you don't put on a condom, you won't get any sensation at all.

Don't worry about birth control. I'll just stay in for a minute.
What do you think I am, a microwave oven?

Sexual Problems and Your Relationship

Many people make themselves unavailable as long-term or marital partners because of sexually related problems. Often, this reaction is hasty and leads to unnecessary discontentment.

For men, the problems usually center on anxiety over sexual performance, resulting in impotence or premature ejaculation. For women, it's mainly fear (or outright terror) of making love, traceable to a traumatic sexual history, perhaps rape, molestation, or simply repeated deception, cruelty, or rejection in past relationships. (Inability to achieve orgasm, in and of itself, is not usually reason enough to dissuade a woman from a relationship or marriage.)

If you have a sex problem, the best approach is to acknowledge your insecurities and anxieties early on in a relationship. If you and your partner like each other, enjoy each other's company, and consider each other potential mates, it's appropriate to be honest about your situation. Say something like, "I want to be up front with you from the very beginning; I have had a problem with sex. My anxiety keeps me from performing the way I want to. I'd like to get close—physically intimate—with you. But I don't want to try having sexual intercourse until I reach a comfort level that permits it."

You'd be surprised how many men and women will find this acceptable. Many couples adapt to this arrangement much more easily than they might to, say, a single experience of impotence, or pain upon attempting intercourse. As we know, the lack of sexual intercourse does not mean that you cannot express your sexuality in other ways. You should also remember that a relationship without sex (even for an extended period) is not necessarily a bitter or unpleasant one; only when one partner feels ignored, ungratified, or unfulfilled does the lack of sexual desire or performance become an issue.

By the way, it is a mistake to assume that men "know it all" in this area. One third of 1,100 women between the ages of 18 and 49 polled recently by *Self* magazine revealed their belief that men are not as good in bed as they think they are. (One can only speculate as to how many of that number shared their perceptions and needs with their partners.)

If your partner has a sex problem, try to remember that the vast majority of sexual disturbances are of psychological origin. (There are, however, some medical exceptions: certain types of impotence, for instance.) As such, the problems are usually subject to cure and even complete recovery. It's your job to assure your partner of this—and to offer patience and flexibility. If you love your partner, it will be worth your while to work the problems out.

Concentrate on developing a sensuous and erotic relationship, not on coitus itself. Try innovative approaches: massage, mutual masturbation, or other ideas from the many books and manuals available today. If, and only if, this approach does not work after a few months, consider professional sex therapy.

Healing the Wounds

Roger is 30; Janice is 23. They are in love. They know it, they can just feel it: they even look right for each other. Everybody says so. They have great times together. They've known each other for three months, and they have not had sex yet. There has been no pressure from Roger, and Janice likes that. Roger has been in this situation before; although Janice has not yet had intercourse, this is by no means her first relationship.

As they get to know each other and become more intimate (still without having sex), Roger seems hesitant somehow, as though he wants to back away. The more Janice opens up to him and shows that she is ready to make a commitment, the more vague and distant Roger becomes. Then, as suddenly as it started, the relationship ends.

Janice is confused and heartbroken; she seeks solace and understanding in psychotherapy. Without ever meeting Roger, her psychiatrist decides, in accordance with his Freudian training, that Roger is a man with a domineering mother in his past, a castration complex in his present psychological state, and an incapacity for any kind of commitment in his foreseeable future.

What Really Went Wrong?

None of this fantasy diagnosis of Roger was accurate. I know, because I learned a lot about Roger when he became one of my patients.

Roger wanted commitment, probably more than anything else in his life. He would have loved to marry Janice. In fact, Roger has a kind and caring mother (as well as a fine, gentle father). That Janice was assertive and independent appealed to him.

Roger's intelligence and sensitivity (the traits that were so attractive to Janice) were genuine. But Roger carried scars from a couple of bad sexual episodes that were left unresolved and that festered for so long that they eventually disrupted his whole life.

What happened? At age 19, Roger could not achieve an erection during his first sexual encounter. This was the first of a sad series of sexual disappointments. All that followed is even more unfortunate in light of the fact that his episode of impotence was probably an idiosyncratic response arising from Roger's drinking too much in hopes of mustering his courage.

After that first encounter, Roger was, in his words, "willing to have sex with someone I did not even like, because I did not want to be the last of the virgins." When Roger finally had sex with someone whom he cared for, he experienced a premature ejaculation.

In short, Roger's early sexual history shows a growing preoccupation with sexual performance. Many men can empathize with his sense of "failing to perform": this is the beginning of the downward spiral that is performance anxiety.

Roger proceeded through a series of relationships, each of which he exited as soon as the reasonable expectation of sex arose. Terrified of the possibility of another sexual humiliation, Roger evaded the problem, but he could not restrain his need to seek the completeness of an intimate human relationship.

The dynamics that accompany this sort of failure by anticipation are much the same for women as for men, but the source of the problems is, generally speaking, different. Due to differences in socialization, women are often pressured to submit where men are pressured to perform. A man can carry scars from the experience of sexual abuse and can have confusion about sexual identity so great that he is fearful about consummating a relationship.

Men and women who want to marry, but who are afraid of sex, should reveal their anxiety to their partner. This calls for courage, but in my experience sensitive men and women who face problems openly can heal each other's wounds. Sexual healing can be an opportunity to develop not only a physical relationship but also the highest forms of friendship, trust, and understanding.

The Penis: Does It Have a Mind of Its Own?

Women are often surprised to learn that many males feel that their penises are not subject to their wishes, that the male genitals are often seen as being "out of control."

In counseling situations, some reveal that they undergo "power struggles" between the penis and will power, frequently attributing to their genitals undesirable attributes unrelated to their conscious intent. "The penis," they've been known to say, "seems to have a mind of its own." (I've been known to say in response, "There is just one mind between you; you had better decide who has it.")

Of course, we are each responsible for our own acts. Men who separate their conscious will from the seemingly independent and often exploitative impulses associated with their genitals are usually engaging in forms of rationalization and denial. When a behavior becomes addictive or involuntary—such as habitual rape or child molestation, or constant preoccupation with pornography—the penis itself may be a convenient scapegoat, and may be assigned the role of the perpetrator, unaccountable and out of control.

In the absence of such rationalizations, however, the idea is not so farfetched. It's true that erections sometimes occur without apparent conscious stimulation (i.e., when a father wrestles with his children, or when a heterosexual man showers with a muscular male friend). Virtually every male has experienced arousal, at some point in his life, without having planned for or encouraged it.

It's not entirely clear just why men have erections associated with events or fantasies that are foreign (or even antithetical) to conscious motives and values, but they do. Men involved in workplace "power play" confrontations with female colleagues have been known to become aroused without any conscious awareness of a sexual interest in the co-worker. Still more curious is the common (but rarely discussed) phenomenon of a man being unwittingly aroused by incest, rape, or dismemberment fantasies that run counter to every basic value he holds.

Strange as such arousals may sound not only to women but to the men who experience them, in the majority of cases they represent no cause for alarm. If these dark urges do not result in inappropriate behavior and are not symptomatic of other neurotic problems, they may simply reflect a normal range of primitive or unconscious sexuality and need not be viewed with concern.

A more serious dilemma stems from the message, which many men receive, that once an erection starts and sexual tension is maintained, there is simply no turning back. Much of what is now identified as date rape is rooted in the erroneous assumption that once a man is sexually aroused, he cannot stop and must act on the arousal. The man may, afterward, blame the woman for encouraging him, often along the lines of, "Well, why did you invite me in?" "You said hello, didn't you?" "Why did you kiss me?" "Why did you give me a drink?" In these instances, as well, rationalization and denial are at the forefront.

Men can stop. The notion that they can't is reinforced in some men by the occurrence of "blue balls" (a pain in the genitals associated with unreleased sexual tension), but masturbation provides instant relief. There is absolutely no physical damage or harm sustained when an aroused man does not "score." The main barrier men in this situation face is the nonsensical and dangerous idea that rape or even sexual molestation is preferable to masturbation.

The organ that really controls the penis is the brain, not the other way around (though it should be recognized that not all aspects of the brain are subject to conscious control). To be sure, there's nothing wrong with a man scolding, waxing philosophical with, or awarding more credit than deserved to his penis. And, as we'll see in the following paragraphs, there's also nothing wrong with masturbating joyfully when the penis seems to be getting the better of an argument.

Masturbation

Masturbation is a healthy, normal outlet for adolescents, adult singles, and even married people (particularly when opportunities for sex with the spouse are temporarily unavailable). Especially when it comes to married couples, however, there remains some resistance to the idea that masturbation can be a part of a well-adjusted sex life. But what are the partners supposed to do when one must, say, go away on a business trip for three weeks? Have affairs? For my money, masturbation represents a far healthier and realistic option in a mature relationship. (It's worth noting, too, that masturbation is the treatment of choice for women who have trouble reaching orgasm.)

Almost all males masturbate at some time during their lives. About three-quarters of women do the same. Nowadays, modern mothers tell their children that it's okay to play with themselves, as long as they do it in private, and not too much. This certainly represents a healthier approach to the matter than was in fashion some years ago (when it was widely believed that "self-abuse" brought in its wake acne, tired blood, heartburn, and, in extreme cases, blindness). But think about it from the child's point of view for a moment: How much is too much? Once a year? Twice a week? After every meal?

The simplest and most honest approach with children is to tell them the truth. Once is too much if you don't like it. If you don't like it, don't do it; otherwise don't worry about it.

As with any activity, masturbation can become neurotic or compulsive. There are people who eat too much because of high anxiety levels, and people who drink too much for the same reason. It would be remarkable indeed if the same weren't true of masturbating.

Granted. Some people do indeed masturbate compulsively, as a response to anxiety. But while many people die every year of excessive drug, alcohol, or food intake, the record has yet to show a case of someone dying from overmasturbation. Masturbation, frankly, is the compulsion of choice, with the highest potential for enjoyment and least harm to oneself or to others. You could call it the cost-effective compulsion.

Although most people in our society grow up with some irrational worries about masturbation, people who are relatively guiltfree when they masturbate find that it relieves tension and inhibits tendencies to act out inappropriate sexual behavior. People who feel masturbation is wrong, by contrast, find it heightens tension and stimulates inappropriate sexual behavior.

If your religion frowns on masturbation, it probably won't do you any harm to avoid it. But please be careful what you tell yourself or your children about self-stimulation. Where people run into genuine problems is not with masturbation itself, but with the guilt that becomes associated with it, particularly when a child is punished for the activity. It's possible for some people to live a celibate life and be happy; I doubt seriously, though, that this can be accomplished if one feels guilt or shame about one's sexuality. In all the work I have done and all the research I have compiled with reference to rape and sexual molestation of children, I have never come across a male perpetrator who didn't feel extremely guilty about masturbation while growing up.

And while we're on that serious subject . . .

If you were sexually molested as a child, you must do whatever is necessary to come to terms with the experience and convince yourself that it was not your fault. The reason for this is simple. It wasn't.

Whether you resisted or not, whether you told someone or not, whether you liked it or not, sexual molestation of children is the responsibility of the adult who initiates it. Always. The adult knows the activity is wrong. The child is the victim.

Unfortunately for the victim, much work remains to be done after the fact. If you fall into this category, you must recover from any guilt feelings and learn not to punish yourself. If you do not recover, you run the risk of becoming a perpetual victim; in a sense, you marry your victimizer. Don't do it. Separate yourself from the victimizer. Living well, as we know, is the best revenge. (Those men who were molested as children must be particularly vigilant about getting help, especially if they have the urge to molest others and thus to perpetuate the tragic cycle of molestation. If you have this tendency, please get help before you hurt anyone—including, of course, yourself.)

The same advice applies to adults who have been raped. The proper mental attitude will go a long way toward helping you deal with the trauma in the healthiest way possible. The rape was not your fault, in just the same way that it would not be your fault if you were mugged. If you need support on your road to recovery (and it is a good bet that you will), you might reach out to help others who have had a similar experience. Join a support group or help in a rape crisis center. Do not punish yourself twice by maintaining an emotional attachment to the person who hurt you.

Homosexuality

About six percent of men are predominantly gay; about four percent of women are predominantly lesbian. No one knows the cause any more than the cause of heterosexuality is known.

As far as we know, a person's sexual orientation is pretty much determined by the time he or she is three to four years old, and that sexual orientation is not a matter of choice.

Many people discover they are homosexual in the late adolescent and early adult years, sometimes after marriage. Some homosexuals marry in an attempt to "cure" themselves, but this rarely, if ever, works.

A few homosexual experiences or fantasies, or the fact that you are approached by a homosexual, does not mean that you are a homosexual. (According to Kinsey, 37 percent of all males have at least one homosexual experience to the point of ejaculation.) What is a homosexual? From a pragmatic point of view, the best definition of homosexual is a person who, as an adult, feels him or herself predominately attracted to, and has sex with, people of the same sex.

These are not easy times to be lesbian or gay. Many extremists have taken public concern over the spread of the AIDS virus as a cue to vent their spleen against homosexuals without fear of encountering mainstream opposition. It is one of the most troubling aspects of contemporary life that many of these extremists spread panic, prejudice, and fear within the context of what they call religion. Bigots, however, will be bigots, even if they hide behind a pulpit.

Most of the logic the extremists offer in defense of their anti-homosexual attitudes simply does not stand scrutiny. When someone argues seriously to me that God has visited His retribution on gays, and that He gave them AIDS as punishment for their immorality, my response is to ask whether God has it in for Legionnaires as well. After all, He gave them Legionnaire's Disease! And if God is so angry at homosexuals, why has He not ensured that lesbians, along with gay men and intravenous drug users, are counted among the major AIDS risk groups?

Safer Sex

Unless you are absolutely sure that both partners are virgins, and utterly confident that neither partner will sleep with someone else while your relationship is going on, I strongly recommend that you use the safer sex methods designed to address the increasingly serious problem of sexually transmitted diseases, including AIDS. (In addition, of course, an intelligent selection of birth control methods will reduce the likelihood of unwanted pregnancy.)

Experts suggest that using the pill or the diaphragm in conjunction with both spermicide and a condom are the safest methods. Though the only completely safe approach to sex is abstinence, there is, today, no excuse for engaging in sexual intercourse without having taken sufficient precautions where health and birth control are concerned.

Here are some other guidelines I recommend you follow if your sex partner is not your long-term monogamous lover.

Avoid anal sex. With or without a condom. (Receptive anal sex represents an activity with the very great risk for transmission of the human immunodeficiency virus—HIV.)

Avoid unprotected oral sex. Or at least stop before ejaculation.

Be sure that neither you nor your partner has sex with prostitutes, intravenous drug users, or bisexual or homosexual males who have had sexual relations in the last ten years. Sexual intercourse with members of high-risk groups increases your chances of contracting the virus. (If you have reasons to doubt your partner's truthfulness, err on the side of caution. A headline in the New York *Times* of August 14, 1988, summed the current situation up accurately: "The Lies Men Tell Put Women in Danger of AIDS.")

Do not engage in one-night stands. Remember that when you sleep with someone casually, you are usually unaware of whether or not his or her partners were in AIDS risk groups; you may be exposing yourself to the virus.

As serious as the AIDS epidemic is, it does not represent the only threat to your health related to sex.

All sexually transmitted diseases require medical treatment, but a special caution is probably in order when discussing herpes. It is estimated that more than thirty million Americans have genital herpes, which, as of today, is an incurable disease. While herpes is most commonly transmitted from a partner who has active lesions, it can also be infectious when there are no obvious symptoms. Therefore, condoms and spermicides should also be used when a partner has herpes, even if there are no visual clues that the lesions are in an active state.

If you have genital herpes, you are strongly urged not to have sex until you've established a mature relationship and informed your partner about the precautions that must be taken. Once the proper steps are followed, there is relatively little risk to the sexual health of someone who sleeps with a person who has herpes. Even before you make love, it's best to be honest early on in the relationship about your condition to avoid later problems.

For more information on how to manage these situations, write: The Herpes Resource Center, P.O. Box 13827, Research Triangle Park, NC 27709 (Enclose a self-addressed business envelope with two first-class stamps.)

Among 65 million sexually active Americans 15 to 34 years old, there will be eight million new cases of sexually transmitted diseases this year. Among them, four million will be chlamydia infections. Women must be aware that they are mainly asymptomatic (i.e., without external signs), for gonorrhea and chlamydia. When these infections go untreated, infertility frequently results. For detailed information, contact your local health department and/or send one dollar to:

American Foundation for the Prevention of Venereal Disease, 799 Broadway, Suite #638, New York, NY 10003 for their excellent pamphlet: Prevention for Everyone. You can also call the STD (sexually transmitted diseases) hot line at (800) 227-8922; or the AIDS hotline at (800) 342-AIDS.

Chapter Nine:
Preparing for the
Responsibility of Family Life—
An Emerging View for
Marriages in the 1990s

WHILE MANY MYTHS and illusions still surround the marital relationship, expectations associated with marriage seem to have become more realistic in recent years. Most couples now realize that when they get married, they are not getting an ideal person but a real person. Reasons for marriage that reach beyond financial security and/or sexual gratification are more common than they were a generation ago. People are more prepared to accept the fact that love will change in intensity, and they are more likely to recognize the need for a couple to work together in order to get through the inevitable difficult periods.

Certainly, no one will deny that these are healthy developments. Over the lifetime of a committed relationship, two people go through periods of indifference and animosity; some marriages even appear to have the effect of moving the partners further apart rather than bringing them closer together. Any long-term relationship, and specifically a marriage, is naturally fluid and changing. If there is a couple whose true feelings never vary from a constantly gleeful state of affection, I have not met them.

Do you remember how intense it felt to be in love at age sixteen? Odds are that, like most people, you were so overwhelmed with the experience that you could not think of anyone other than your beloved and could not bear the shortest separation without distress. You may have had difficulty sleeping. But those kinds of strong feelings during adolescence tend to last for only a short time. The "undying love" dies and is, in short order, replaced by a new "undying love." That process, while it can be embarrassing in retrospect, is an essential part of growing up.

Unfortunately, there are still too many people who marry with the notion that their honeymoon can last forever. Trying to turn this initial rush of "undying love" into a permanent home environment is so unrealistic that it binds a couple to a perpetual source of disappointment and frustration.

Moments of Joy

The most meaningful experiences in life are brief. Consider the things you enjoy most—orgasms, sunsets, a child's first steps. How long do they last? Just imagine how bored and exhausted you would be if you actually made the superhuman effort necessary to attempt to prolong the intensity of those activities day after day. And imagine how unnatural and empty the experience would be if you could somehow succeed in doing so.

Marriage is the same way. There are moments of dissatisfaction. And there are moments of joy.

Many couples who've been married for a long time complain that their intimacies have become monotonous and that their feelings for each other are no longer exciting. Perhaps they have fallen into the routine of making love at certain hours; at a fixed interval.

For some, the act has lost its imaginative quality and become a mechanical repetition of worn-out positions and techniques.

Other couples, married just as long, are able to bring moments of spontaneity and joy to lovemaking that allow them to relive the joy of their commitment. They may not make love five times a week, but they sustain the excitement and intensity of their private moments.

Myths

Some people would have you believe that marital love and companionship within the strict limits of the pair-bond should satisfy an individual's every emotional, physical, social, and intellectual need. Couples who try to live this myth share all the same friends and discard those who don't get along with both partners, abandon long-held interests or hobbies because the spouse does not share them, and generally maintain "the couple front" wherever they go. They signal to all outsiders that each partner is off limits to any activity unless both show enthusiasm for it.

While sharing *no* interests and spending little time together is equally harmful, at the opposite extreme, the "couple trap" I just outlined is not recommended for any relationship. Complete possessiveness in the name of love has two troubling effects. First, it stifles individual expression and creativity. Second, it places limitations on a couple's range of experience. Shared *values* are crucial; identical *interests* are not.

Almost all of us depend upon other people for our emotional and physical well-being. Within the framework of the more overburdened and overdependent relationships, however, dependency can result in unrealistic expectations and, often, a seemingly endless source of hurt feelings. Partners realize before long that one person simply cannot mean everything.

Toward Egalitarian Marriages

Some men say they like a traditional marriage setting—one with rigidly defined gender roles—because each partner knows what has to be done. And there is a regularity to these marriages: the husband works, the wife handles most of the domestic duties. But intimacy and caring frequently evaporate. When a marriage is reduced to a series of chores, it often becomes nothing more. Many of these men reserve Monday as their football night, Tuesday as their bowling night, Wednesday as their night out with the boys, and so on. They're just not around a lot. They find their marriages boring, and because they think that all marriages are boring, they are unwilling to work to change things.

These men avoid contact in any number of ways. They may still have sex with their wives, but they are rarely intimate. Many of these wives feel that their roles in such marriages are unchallenging and repetitive, that there are few accepted avenues for self-expression in *their* rigidly defined lives. (On the other hand, traditional marriages do work for many men and women, despite the unflattering generalizations I have just put forth. You see this sometimes among religious couples who genuinely respect each other's roles, however rigidly those roles may be defined.)

Slowly, society moves more and more toward egalitarian marriages, toward settings that encourage differences in taste and opinion without threatening the core of the relationship—intimacy and commitment.

Today's thoughtful marriage partners must confront the fact that life is not automatically exciting—and that having fun is a privilege accorded to those who are willing to think creatively about their surroundings. A mutual resolve to make the daily routine more of a surprise for both partners will go a long way toward providing marital stability and happiness.

Conflict

Occasional antagonism between spouses is a fact of life. Yet people often become extremely defensive and anxious when told that their mate can be expected to go through periods of indifference (or even hate) over the course of a long relationship.

The higher your expectation is that conflict will never arise, the deeper your disappointment will be when it does. Those seemingly inconsequential resentments and frustrations we refuse to bring into the light often resurface—disguised as hardened, uncompromising attitudes—and can cast a shadow of hostility over the relationship.

It's best to accept the fact that your marriage will have good days and bad days, and that occasional fights are *healthy* components of any relationship. In the long run, if your relationship is a mature one, your partner will be around next week even if he or she was out of sorts this morning.

Goodbye to the Stereotypes, But . . .

The strict gender-based social roles, which used to set the terms of most marriages, are rapidly becoming things of the past. This is a healthy development that promises to help bring variety, challenge, and long-term fulfillment to a greater percentage of marriages than ever before.

While the stereotypes may be on their way out, many of the attitudes that supported them remain. Optimally, marital responsibility is based on a mutual desire to meet the other partner's needs. If you learn to view your spouse's needs as demands, you aren't likely to enjoy fulfilling them.

If you demand that I cook your favorite meal and threaten to withhold a similar pleasure unless I comply, I will begrudge you the favor. But if I am asked in a pleasant manner—if you speak to me as though you were addressing an equal, not an idiot or errant child—we'll both enjoy ourselves. I'll make the meal, not because I have to, but because I enjoy doing so and because I love you. Pleasing each other thus becomes an opportunity for mutual giving, not an act of submission or conquest.

Along the same lines, helping around the house is no fun when it descends into the deadening realm of the expected. If it is always one person's turn to clean the cat box, and if that person finds the task distasteful (as most anyone would), then after a while the fetid cat box will become a source of genuine resentment. This cycle, of course, does nothing to make a necessary job more pleasant. Agreeing to alternate tasks (even if you've had a hard day when your turn comes around) will help remove the monotony of domestic duties. Such changes, though they tend to focus on little things, can bring new zest and interest to a marriage.

Try to promote a sense of equality. When men and women can come together as equals (not as provider/consumer or leader/follower), they improve their relationships. The best environment for growth is one in which each partner feels as competent and in control of life as the other.

Marriage: Out of Style?

Many contemporary commentators question the future of the institution of marriage. Some claim that the duration of even meaningful relationships is becoming, on average, shorter. The reasons cited include people's increased tendency to move frequently, the fact that many of us hold our jobs for shorter periods of time than our parents did, and the rapidly changing values and interests of people in our society.

Perhaps intimacy and really getting to know other people *are* more difficult these days. Certainly there has been a proliferation of short-term relationships, many with the professed goal of getting the "barrier" of sex out of the way early on. And it is perhaps a little too fashionable these days to make excuses or convincing rationalizations for infidelity or adultery.

In this area, generalization is not profitable. No rigid notions of what relationships are or are not going through can fully account for each couple's uniqueness. There are people in monogamous relationships of thirty or forty years' duration who are positively loveless and hateful towards each other; there are a fair number of not entirely faithful couples who love each other a great deal.

No matter how fast-paced or challenging the demands of today's world become, there is nothing inherently boring about monogamy. If you put in the time and caring required to allow mutual trust to grow in your marriage, the relationship will make you happy and keep you interested. Once you and your partner have developed good communication skills, together you can satisfy most of the needs you identify.

Step-parenting

If you marry a divorced or widowed person, step-parenting could be in your future. Step-parents must often play a challenging role in today's families, particularly when the biological parent is still alive (as is usually the case). If you are about to enter this situation, there are a number of problems you may encounter.

Though there are undoubtedly many, many families that integrate a step-parenting situation successfully, as a general rule step-parents face tougher challenges than other family members.

Step-parenting is *not* just like being a normal parent, nor is it equivalent to adopting a child. A step-mother or step-father who tries to adjust to an existing family unit faces a far different situation than just about any other type of relative; specifically, the step-parent must confront the fact that others may perceive him or her as a replacement, and deal with the (understandable) resentment that often accompanies this perception.

Here are some tips that will help you approach the experience of step-parenting, and can assist you in making the transition into a fulfilling, satisfying family life.

You can expect that the children will usually harbor some resentment, and will consciously or unconsciously try to put you on the defensive and test your limits. It's not reasonable to expect a child to understand fully the situation that led to the divorce or death of the "real" parent. Unfavorable comparisons are to be expected.

In addition, your step-children may have feelings of resentment or anger stemming from the perception that you, a relative newcomer, now appear to have priority when it comes to your partner's time, affection, or money. Some step-children even cross the line between passive dissatisfaction and make active attempts to cause the marriage to fail. Such efforts may be sparked by presumed unequal treatment by the new parent, but sometimes over something as seemingly trivial as a new living arrangement (which might, for instance, force two children to share what had been one person's room). There are also the difficult instances in which a child tries to make a marriage fail in hope of seeing his parents reunited.

One point frequently overlooked is that children as a whole, and step-children in particular, are, like all of us, influenced by genetic as well as environmental factors. These factors can influence a child in ways that the step-parent may not always be able to control or understand. Some children will never feel love for the new parent (just as some step-parents will not be able to feel love for some children). In these cases, "trying hard" becomes an academic concern; love cannot be mandated. Failing to accept such circumstances can lead to unnecessary feelings of guilt or rage; in many families, inappropriate behavior such as overaggressiveness, contempt, or pity may follow.

In general, it is best to operate on the assumption that the child does not have to love you or even like you. It's good to keep this in mind at all times, but it's especially important when dealing with direct challenges along the lines of, "You're not my mother (father). I don't have to love you!" (Of course, no one is saying that dealing with such situations will be easy.) Your best response to such an outburst may be something like this:

> You do not have to love me or even like me, but you do have to treat me with respect, because I have enough self-respect to say NO to abuse. And you will also notice that I have enough self-respect to respect you. I think that it will be more pleasurable for all of us if we try to get along better.

When, as a step-parent, you must play the role of the disciplinarian, you will have to walk a fine line. Do not require that the step-child obey you out of respect for your authority or love for you as a family member; you can't count on either one existing, particularly in the early stages. And *never* give in to the temptation to use threats like, "If you don't take out the garbage, I'm telling your father!"

Questions Step-parents Ask . . .
and Some Possible Answers

Sometimes I feel such mixed emotions from my step-children. One minute they hug me and the next minute they give me the cold shoulder. How should I handle this?

Remember, you are the adult. They are the kids. Even if our emotions never grow up, our actions must. It hurts, but we must accept it. This is the real world, and sometimes people's emotions are in conflict. If you feel this represents a lasting problem, you might bring it up at a time when the child is feeling affectionate towards you.

My four-year-old step-son recently looked up at me and said: "My mommy says you're not my real step-mother until she dies." I didn't know what to say. Do you?

How about, "That's right, dear. She is your real mother, but we both love you."

How can I minimize the initial tension that builds up in the first hour or so when my step-children visit for the weekend?

Arrange for activities (such as movies, games, or visits with friends) that don't require you to make conversation. Let the relationship and the discussions develop at their own pace.

Why do I sometimes feel that I have to do better than my step- children's real mother?

Why you feel that way is not as important as how you deal with the feeling. Tell yourself, "I'll do the best I can." Of course, recognizing the competitiveness is the first (and perhaps most important) step.

I married a woman with three kids . . . my first marriage. Lately, my wife has been subtly putting pressure on me to play my part in the "one big happy family" cast. I think she's trying to compensate for what was missing from her last marriage. I understand what she is trying to do, but it's making me resent the kids and I have begun pushing her away, too. What should I do?

Suggest to your wife that her efforts are not realistic, but make every effort to maintain a good, genuine relationship with the kids. Why punish them? If the situation seems to be deteriorating, counseling would probably be the best approach.

I'm planning to marry a woman with two children. They want to call me Dad, but I don't feel that I'm ready for that. Any suggestions?

Let them call you Dad. Seriously, what's the big deal? The problem is usually the other way around—children are often understandably hesitant in reassigning their affections. As an adult in the family, you should be willing to make some compromises. If you really feel it's a problem, talk to them. But such issues are more important, in the long run, to the children than to you. Try to let them decide; give the situation time.

Everyone Learns

There's no denying that step-parenting can be difficult. By the same token, the family that incorporates a step-parent enjoys unique opportunities for growth on the part of both the parents and children. Children may have additional adult role models to whom they can look for guidance and motivation. The act of creatively resolving the inevitable conflicts can be a learning experience for everyone in the family. Furthermore, dual-family situations, in which there are more than the customary two parents, allow for a domestic environment in which no parent has a monopoly on providing for all emotional or financial needs.

Even bearing all this in mind, you may still approach the prospect of entering someone else's family with some trepidation. Luckily, if you plan to become a step-parent, you are not alone. One or more children living with a step-parent and a natural parent is a characteristic household in about ten percent of all American families; it's estimated that there are some twelve million step-parents in the United States. It's likely that you have a friend or relative in a parallel situation to whom you can turn for more advice.

How Not to Define Love . . .
And How to Teach Your Children
Once You've Finished Not Defining It

Many people try to nail down exactly what love means so they can use the definition to help them find the solutions to problems in their marriages or relationships. The efforts are usually fruitless.

The popular formula "Love is . . ." is nothing more than a catch phrase popular with writers and speakers eager to capitalize on the public's hunger for easy answers to difficult questions. The very fact that hundreds of phrases have been used to complete the sentence should give some indication of the difficulty in providing a truly authoritative definition.

Love is not an ending point. It's a starting point. To love truly, you have to start by loving yourself. Believe that you are a worthwhile human being with valid feelings, thoughts, and behaviors that you accept. It is absolutely essential that this be the first step of any love relationship. If you don't believe others can love you, you'll believe that you have no love to give.

It follows that instilling a healthy sense of self-worth is the first step we can take in passing along a realistic view of love to our children. There are a number of ways to do this, but these are among the most important:

Remind yourself that the child has a valid point of view and legitimate opinions. Your child may lack maturity, but that does not mean there is any lack of insight into things that matter to him or her. Try to listen, not just issue demands, ultimatums, and rules.

Don't tell the child what to feel or what to want. We have already identified this as a condescending and futile approach to a partner; the effect is the same when it's applied to children (i.e., it doesn't work).

Do not belittle the child. This world provides sufficient reasons for self-criticism; do not spend energy giving your child added cause for self-doubt. Be particularly careful when adolescence dawns and your son or daughter makes his or her first attempts at love. Don't use words like phase or puppy love in describing these relationships; experimental or awakening love are better terms. The best response is no comment at all unless your opinion is invited.

Don't criticize your child for things he or she cannot change. This can lead to feelings of inadequacy.

Don't push your child to excel in areas where he or she has no interest and/or talent. If there is anything worse than not doing something well, it's being coerced to do something that you cannot do well.

Praise your child's uniqueness in small ways every day. Don't go overboard; do just enough to remind the child that there is no one else exactly like him or her.

Answer your child's questions about sex. If you can help integrate a child's sexuality into his or her personhood (instead of denying that sex exists or compartmentalizing it as some clandestine or unmentionable part of existence), you will have done your part in providing your child with a healthy sex education.

In an egalitarian relationship, both partners know there is mutual commitment to a clearly defined list of priorities, developed to foster the growth of their relationship and of the individual people in it. There's no reason that the partners' same thoughtful plan cannot be extended to their children. The items I have outlined above represent a good starting point.

There are few people who can be content with the love of a young child in place of a partner's love. As a rule, marriage partners are lovers before they are parents; affections for one's partner will not disappear when a child is born, nor will needs for support and love. Thankfully, love is not an inflexible, mathematical constant: With a little adjustment to the new environment, most couples discover what worked for two will, in time make three (or more) very happy.

Perhaps the most difficult part about raising children is identifying where your parental authority ends and your child's rights as an individual begin. Establishing this elusive line should not be a continually threatening and unpleasant experience—but the line must be drawn so that it can lead to respect for privacy and self-determination.

In the end, no matter how hard parents try to communicate honestly and set correct guidelines, they must accept that they do not have absolute control over their child's development and, indeed, that they should not try to win such control. Like it or not, you will not be the only influence your child will encounter.

What, then, should we teach our children? Responsibility to themselves and responsibility to others. That we are there for them when they need our help and our love. Finally, that as they love themselves, they will learn to love others.

Chapter Ten:
Self-Acceptance—
The Cornerstone

THERE HAS BEEN A FLOOD of books exhorting you to feel good about yourself. Most of their advice fits a pattern. Forget the past, they advise; forget the guilt, just deal with the present. Forget about unpleasant things like retribution, or the fact that you've come down with a terminal illness and have six months to live. Just imagine yourself in a miraculous, joyful existence, forgive everyone who has ever hurt you, accept who you are now, and you will be all you ever dreamed of being.

All of which is hogwash. The plain fact is that life, in large measure, is made up of things to worry about. Not only personal things, like family, career, or relationship problems, but also problems relating to the state of the world in which we live, a world that must confront unpleasant realities like war, hunger, over-population, torture, urban disintegration, drought and flood, famine, disease, and death. To be joyful in the face of all this is not done by flipping a switch in your head but by striving to live up to realistic expectations, doing your share in making this world a better place to live, and rededicating yourself to do better when you fail. There is nothing wrong with creative visualization as a meditation tool, but nothing changes until you change the way you act toward your fellow creatures on planet earth.

Life can be unfair, unlucky, uninteresting, or unnerving for extended periods of time. Real people, accordingly, have bad moods, periods of depression, and episodes of unrequited love. By the same token, life can also be full of joy, pleasure, and excitement. Even if such experiences are short-lived, they are valid.

The injunction simply to forgive everyone is not based in real-life experience. There's no need to be hostile to all those who have hurt you, but for most people emotional battle lines are not so clearly drawn as to allow blanket pardons. Forgiveness is better defined as a direction than an objective. Some people will be easy to forgive; others will have to settle for understanding, rather than complete acceptance; still others will retain a claim on some of our anger, even though we know that hostility, as a rule, is not energy efficient.

I will not ask you to pretend that yours is the only reality or that you live in a perfect world. My message is this: Accept yourself as you are. Visualize the self you can become. And, though you must acknowledge the pain of the real world, renew and revitalize yourself by reaching out beyond your own pain to help others.

Sometimes, to be sure, you will feel guilty. If you do something wrong (as any human being can be expected to), you should try to learn from your mistakes and remedy the situation to the best of your ability. Then drop it. Try not to make the mistake of feeling guilty irrationally or punishing yourself beyond reason. Accept yourself. In time, you will acquire wisdom without even trying. In time, you'll become comfortable with a healthy level of daydreaming about your future and spend less time castigating yourself. And in time, you'll be willing to take risks with others. Each of these achievements will open up exciting new possibilities for you.

Feeling Good About Yourself:
What It Does Not Mean

Watch out for people who feel so good about themselves that they have no qualms about riding roughshod over your feelings.

Feeling good about yourself is no excuse for selfish, greedy, or uncaring behavior. You would be surprised how many people come away from the new-age, quack-cure-yourself, instant-fix, you-are-your-own-salvation workshops feeling good about themselves and being plain mean to everybody else. That is not the kind of feeling good I mean. The kind I am talking about leaves you with more energy, higher levels of optimism, and a willingness to be nice to the majority of the people with whom you come into contact.

Obviously, there is more to developing healthy self-esteem than spending day after day in ecstasy. (If that were the objective, drug abuse, which can bring brief periods of ecstasy, would be the path to ultimate happiness.) Human beings have ups and downs. Well-adjusted people feel depressed when something depressing happens. But they won't marry their depression or allow themselves to fixate on images of an awful world for days on end. They will work through it.

Effective people have usually developed what is called self-acceptance: the ability to distinguish rational from irrational thoughts and, most important, the ability to separate rational criticism of one's behavior from healthy acceptance of oneself as a person. Self-acceptance mandates that we accept some connection with the humanity of all human beings, good and evil, and that is not easy. But such acceptance makes it possible to make the best of being yourself.

To be sure, humans are fallible: we make mistakes. It's up to us to turn those mistakes into lessons. If we've experienced a failure, such as a marriage that didn't work out, we recognize the reality of the situation. The marriage failed. But a self-accepting person will know that the fact that the marriage was a failure is no indication that the people involved are now failures.

Chapter Eleven: Summing Up

THIS IS THE END of the book, but perhaps you still have doubts about the relationship in your future. That's all right. No one is claiming that finding and keeping a mature relationship is an exact science, or that writing an exact, all-purpose definition of maturity is possible. There will be times when you feel uncertain about what you should do next.

Thankfully, there are guidelines you can follow. The first one is simple:

Be gentle with yourself. Make sure that you are moving towards your ideal of becoming someone with whom it is worthwhile to spend time.

Once you see that you are working with yourself, there are questions you can ask about your relationship with another person. The following observation points will help you determine whether or not you are on the right track.

If you find that your partner consistently makes you feel bad about yourself, or if you find that when you have a fight in the morning, you end up spending the rest of the day recovering from the abuse, then you have signals that you are involved in an immature relationship. Similarly, if you feel good about yourself only in the presence of your partner, or if you seem, as a result of the relationship, not to care about the rest of the world or the feelings of others, the odds are that the relationship is immature. And chances are that an immature relationship is not going to make you happy in the long run.

But if you are in the kind of relationship that makes you feel good, both when you are with your partner and when you're apart, the kind of relationship that reinforces your acceptance of yourself without draining your mate, the kind of relationship that leaves you feeling happy at the end of the day, as if you had found your place in the world, then congratulations. You are involved in a challenging, growth-oriented, mature relationship. Keep growing!

The Secret

Permit me to conclude with an autobiographical note.

I'm past sixty-seven years old, yet I am far from retiring. As I travel around the country, people say I give very lively lectures. Often I am asked, "Where on earth do you get so much energy?"

Allow me to let you in on a secret.

When I began my professional career about 45 years ago, I was out to save the world. I tried that for a few years, without much success. I was getting depressed. Eventually I came to the conclusion that I might have taken on too much. So I decided to save the United States.

After a few years of intense work, I didn't have much to show for my efforts. I was crestfallen. Had I been on the wrong track from the very beginning? I resolved to save my neighborhood.

My neighbors did not appreciate my zeal. Furious, they usually told me to mind my own business.

I considered the possibility of going to Harvard to earn an MBA. When I decided I wasn't that desperate, I vowed to redouble my efforts, and to work on saving my own family. I was forced to accept, finally, that I was having a hard time doing that.

Through all the experiences, I learned something about humility. I learned that I could not be a hero in somebody else's situation. I could only be me in my situation.

Sometimes, when I get depressed, I turn to the Talmud (a commentary on the Old Testament). One day, as I was reading, a miracle took place. As though written for me, the Talmud proclaimed: "If you can save one person, it is as though you have saved the world."

When they teach the golden rule (you know: "Do unto others as you would have them do unto you,") they always leave out the best part: "It's your move."

One person. One at a time.

That is my secret. That is the key to leading a meaningful life and to having more than enough energy.

If this book saves one person, if it makes the world a better place for one reader, it will have served its purpose. And I will have done my mitzvah.

If you are the one reader I have helped, good. Now it's your turn. Do a mitzvah. Don't ask anyone's permission (they usually say no). Just do it.

And you know what else is nice about mitzvah therapy? You meet the nicest people along the way.

Appendix

For practical people at the point of making the decision to marry or not to marry, I suggest that you take a look at the following quiz.

QUESTIONNAIRE
For the Married and for Those Approaching Marriage

How do you feel about your potential marriage partner, or your spouse?

Too often people are insecure about their relationships. They wonder: Is this relationship worth nurturing and preserving, or should I terminate it? I suggest that the following ten questions measure your opinion of the ten critical areas of any relationship and that your answers offer a basis for you to evaluate the current state of your relationship.

A basically secure relationship is not affected by whether or not one has children, whether one has little money or lots of it, or whether one works inside or outside the home. The key to good rapport is where one places one's priorities. I am not speaking of exclusivity here. Priority means that your partner's needs are more important than other people's needs. Buddies, depression, alcohol, television, or other activities can adversely affect a person's priorities and consequently interfere in that person's relationship.

I am suggesting that the following ten areas are crucial aspects of a relationship, more or less in order of importance. Write the answers on separate sheets of paper—but don't share your responses while you are taking the test. Circle the number that in your judgment reflects the current state of the relationship. The lowest number reflects the poorest, while the highest reflects an ideal score. Try to avoid the highest number unless you feel the area deserves an almost perfect rating. Respond to each question separately, then total the score.

Use this exercise as an opportunity to communicate with each other about discrepancies in the responses. Remember, it is as easy to attack and to criticize as it is to distort the score.

This test is worthwhile only if used to open discussions, review current events, renew perspectives on each other, reeducate yourselves on your mate's tendencies, or (last but not least) to reinvigorate your sense of humor.

Ten Key Relationship Questions

1. Loving, caring, respecting each other. Available in times of hardship, loneliness, and grief as well as periods of joy. Remembering birthdays and anniversaries. Are you sensitive to each other's needs?

   1.....2.....3.....4.....5.....6.....7.....8.....9.....10

   Poor   Needs Some Improvement   Great

2. A sense of humor: without it life becomes gray, a real drag. William James suggested that "wisdom is learning what to overlook." Laugh a little. None of us is perfect. (I am certainly not suggesting that you make fun of each other's vulnerabilities.) Do you laugh with each other?

1.....2.....3.....4.....5.....6.....7.....8.....9.....10

Poor   Needs Some Improvement   Great

3. Communication. People say that if you see a man and a woman together at a resort and they are not talking to each other, they must be married. Or, if they are talking to each other, they may be married, but not to each other. Are you able to have conversations that range from significant to playful? I am not suggesting that even the most mature couples tell all. Sometimes honesty is a way of expressing hostility. When you talk to your partner, does the conversation have a sense of zip and enthusiasm?

1.......2.......3.......4.......5.......6.......7.......8

Poor   Needs Some Improvement   Great

4. Trust and security. Are you able to count on the other person?

1.......2.......3.......4.......5.......6.......7.......8

Poor   Needs Some Improvement   Great

5. Tolerance for occasional moodiness, depression, craziness, and the ability not to bear a grudge. How capable are you of dealing with the unharmonious aspects of the relationship?

1.........2.........3.........4.........5.........6

Poor   Needs Some Improvement   Great

6. Ability to share major interests, such as religion, politics, recreation, doing mitzvahs. Do you share common interests?

1.........2.........3.........4.........5.........6

Poor   Needs Some Improvement   Great

7. Ability to respect differences. Even when your partner has friends you don't like, you can have some friends separately. Can he (or she) have interests that don't interest you?

1.........2.........3.........4.........5.........6

Poor   Needs Some Improvement   Great

8. Excitement in planning for future events. Vacations, organizing an event, decorating the house, throwing a party. Do you enjoy doing what you do together?

1.........2.........3.........4.........5.........6

Poor   Needs Some Improvement   Great

9. Sexual fulfillment. Is your sex-life mutually satisfying?

1.........2.........3.........4.........5.........6

Poor   Needs Some Improvement   Great

10. Sharing household tasks. Do you or will you share households chores?

1.....2.....3.....4.....5.....6.....7.....8.....9

Poor   Needs Some Improvement   Great

How to Use Your Results

A perfect score of 73 points means your partner is an illusion or your perceptions are weak.

A score of between 55 and 63 or more points means that the relationship is in good shape. Here, any category rated poor should be discussed.

A score of between 45 and 55 points probably means that some tensions exist, but they are not necessarily disruptive. This is not a good score if you are not yet married. Work on these discrepancies before you decide to marry.

Under 45: have easy talks. Try to communicate and resolve your differences. If this process brings about an argument, see a counselor. Almost any relationship is salvageable with mutual good intentions.

I have not gathered scientific data to justify my positions, but I can think of no better way of getting couples to talk to each other about critical issues.

Recommended Reading

Here are some of the most helpful books I have come across dealing with the topics of self-esteem, relationships, sexuality, and long-term personal growth. If you have time or desire to read only ten books over the next year, reach for the stars (*); I've placed asterisks next to the ten books I consider most helpful.

Barbach, Lonnie. *For Each Other: Sharing Sexual Intimacy*. Signet, 1984.

Bessell, Harold. *The Love Test*. Warner, 1984.

* Boston Women's Health Book Collective. *The New Our Bodies, Our Selves*. Simon & Schuster, 1984.

Buscaglia, Leo. *Living, Loving, and Learning*. Fawcett, 1983.

* Cassell, Carol. *Swept Away: Why Women Fear Their Own Sexuality*. Fireside, 1989.

Cohen, Sara Kay. *Whoever Said Life Was Fair? A Guide to Growing Through Life's Injustices*. Berkley, 1984.

Colton, Helen. *Touch Therapy*. Zebra, 1985.

Comfort, Alex. *More Joy of Sex*. Crown, 1987.

Cowan, Connel, and Kinder, Melvyn. *Women Men Love—Women Men Leave*. Signet, 1987.

Crewsdon, J. *By Silence Betrayed: Sexual Abuse of Children in America*. Little, Brown, 1988.

Dodson, Betty. *Sex for One: The Joy of Selfloving*. Crown, 1987.

* Ellis, Albert. *How To Stubbornly Refuse to Make Yourself Miserable About Anything—Yes, Anything*. Lyle Stuart, 1988.

Farrell, Warren. *Why Men Are the Way They Are*. Berkley, 1988.

* Frankl, Victor. *Man's Search for Meaning*. Touchstone, 1984.

Fromm, Erich. *The Art of Loving*. Bantam, 1956.

Gaylin, Willard. *Rediscovering Love*. Penguin. 1987.

Gordon, Sol. *Seduction Lines Heard 'Round the World and Answers You Can Give*. Prometheus, 1987.

* Gordon, Sol. *When Living Hurts*. Dell, 1988.

Gordon, Sol, and Gordon, Judith. *Raising a Child Conservatively in a Sexually Permissive World*. Fireside, 1989.

Gordon, Sol, and Snyder, Craig. *Personal Issues in Human Sexuality (2d ed.)*. Allyn & Bacon, 1989.

* Gordon, Sol, and Brecher, Harold. *Life Is Uncertain; Eat Dessert First*. Delacorte, 1990.

Greenberg, Martin. *The Birth of a Father*. Avon, 1986.

Harayda, Janice. *The Joy of Being Single*. Doubleday, 1986.

* Hazelton, L. *The Right to Feel Bad: Coming to Terms with Normal Depression*. Dial Press, 1984.

Hochschild, Arlie. *The Second Shift*. Viking, 1989.

Hoffman, Susanna. *Men Who Are Good For You and Men Who Are Bad*. Ten Speed Press, 1987.

Klagsbrun, F. *Married People: Staying Together in the Age of Divorce*. Bantam, 1985.

Klein, Marty. *Your Sexual Secrets*. Berkley Press, 1990.

* Kushner, Harold S. *When Bad Things Happen to Good People*. Avon, 1983.

Lasswell, Marcia, and Lobsenz, Norman. *Styles of Loving.* Ballantine, 1984.

Lazarus, Arnold A. *Marital Myths.* Impact, 1985.

Leight, Lynn. *Raising Your Child to Be Sexually Healthy.* Avon, 1990.

Masters and Johnson, with Kolodny. *On Sex and Human Loving.* Little, Brown, 1986.

McCarthy, B., and McCarthy, E. *Sexual Awareness: Enhancing Sexual Pleasure.* Carroll & Graff, 1984.

McCoy, Kathleen. *Coping with Single Parenting.* NAL, 1987.

McNaught, Brian. *On Being Gay.* St. Martins, 1988.

Nelson, James B. *Between Two Gardens: Reflections on Sexuality and Religious Experience.* Pilgrim Press, 1988.

Nelson, James B. *The Intimate Connection: Male Sexuality, Masculine Spirituality.* Westminster Press, 1988.

Olds, S. W. *The Eternal Garden: Secrets of Our Sexuality.* Times, 1985.

Paul, Jordan, and Paul, Margaret. *Do I Have to Give Up Me to Be Loved by You?* Compcare, 1985.

Paul, Jordan, and Paul, Margaret, with Hesse, Bonnie. *If You Really Loved Me . . .* Compcare, 1987.

Peck, M. Scott. *The Different Drum.* Simon & Schuster, 1987.

* Peck, M. Scott. *The Road Less Traveled.* Simon & Schuster, 1978.

Prather, Hugh and Gayle. *Book for Couples.* Doubleday, 1988.

* Shiff, Eileen (ed.). *Experts Advise Parents*. Delacorte, 1988.

Sullivan, S. K., and Kawiak, M. A. *Parents Talk Love: A Family Handbook About Sexuality*. Bantam, 1988.

Twerksi, Abraham. *Like Yourself and Others Will, Too*. Prentice- Hall, 1986.

Viorst, Judith. *Necessary Losses*. Fawcett, 1986.

Wanderer, Zev, and Fabian, Erika. *Making Love Work*. Ballantine, 1978.

Index

Why Men Commit
Susan Kelley
ISBN 1-55850-159-2, $6.95, 188 pages
Trade paperback

Why does a man decide to commit to a relationship?

In *Why Men Commit*, Susan Kelley reveals the intriguing results of her extensive nationwide survey about why men choose a particular mate. She shows what men seek in a lifetime partner (it's not a great body), and how they change perspective when approaching marriage for the second time.

Men don't marry for the reasons most women think they do, and it is the women who understand this, the ones who know how to approach the issue of commitment with a man, who achieve enriching lifelong relationships.

- What do men think about long-term relationships?
- What are the characteristics of a man who won't commit, no matter what?
- What should you say — and avoid saying — when you want to make a lasting commitment?

30 Secrets of Happily Married Couples

Dr. Paul Coleman
ISBN 1-55850-166-5, $7.95, 188 pages
Trade paperback

Dr. Paul Coleman has studied hundreds of couples and discovered that the strongest and happiest marriages share 30 distinct traits. This book outlines these secrets of happily married couples, and provides reallife examples of how to use the techniques.

Happy couples know the importance of:

- Not always compromising
- Balancing Logic and emotion
- Knowing how and when to forgive
- Uncovering hidden agendas
- Knowing when to keep quiet, and when not to

You don't have to be unhappy in your marriage to wish it could be happier. You can have a committed, caring relationship but still be weary of the complacency, frustrated by a partner's personality quirks. Its better to change your relationship than try to change your partner, and this book shows you 30 proven ways to do just that.

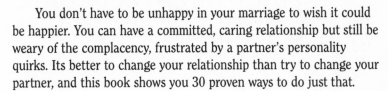

Available Wherever Books Are Sold

If you cannot find these titles at your favorite retail outlet, you may order them directly from the publisher. BY PHONE: Call 1-800-872-5627. We accept Visa, Mastercard, and American Express. $4.95 will be added to your total order for shipping and handling. BY MAIL: Write out the full titles of the books you'd like to order and send payment, including $4.95 for shipping and handling, to: Adams Media Corporation, 260 Center Street, Holbrook, MA 02343. 30-day money-back guarantee.

Why Men Stray, Why Men Stay

Susan Kelley
Trade paperback, 176 pages
1-55850-634-9, $9.95

In *Why Men Stray, Why Men Stay*, men get to say what's really on their minds. And once you know what men are really looking for–as well as the warning signs that can signal trouble on the horizon–you'll know how to make sure that your relationship is one of the exceptional few that survive. Whether you're married or single, having trouble in your relationship, or just hoping to avoid it–or if you're just baffled by the way men act-this book is for you!

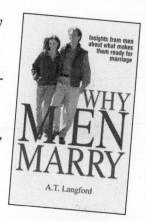

About the Author

Sol Gordon received his B.A. and M.S. from the University of Illinois in 1947, and his Ph.D. in psychology from the University of London in 1953. He has since served as the Chief Psychologist at the Philadelphia Child Guidance Clinic and the Middlesex County Mental Health Clinic. Dr. Gordon taught at Yeshiva University; he was Professor of Child and Family Studies and Director of the Institute for Family Research and Education at Syracuse University. He has written fifteen books and over one hundred articles, and now devotes his time to group lectures and seminars on such topics as sexuality, the promotion of self-esteem, and suicide prevention.